Singing Games

Singing Games
For Families, Schools and Communities

by
Anna Rainville

with illustrations by
Helen Caswell and Lee Anne Welch

Rudolf Steiner College Press

Publication of this book was made possible by a grant
from the Waldorf Curriculum Fund.

Musical transcription and pen and ink drawings: Lee Anne Welch
Full page illustrations: Helen Caswell
Cover art: Helen Caswell
Cover design: Claude Julien and John Wihl

ISBN 0-945803-78-8

Printed by Sierra Copy & Printing, Sacramento, California

The content of this book represents the view of the author and should
not be taken as the official opinion or policy of Rudolf Steiner College
or Rudolf Steiner College Press.

Book orders may be made through Rudolf Steiner College Bookstore.
Tel: 916-961-8729 Fax: 916-961-3032
Catalog and online orders: www.steinercollege.edu
E-mail: bookstore@steinercollege.edu

Rudolf Steiner College Press
9200 Fair Oaks Blvd.
Fair Oaks, CA 95628, U.S.A.

To my family
A.R.

To my parents
L.W.

To my grandchildren
H.C.

Acknowledgments

From the Author
I would like especially to thank my parents, Betty and Willys Peck, and Sarah, Merina and Don Rainville. Their love and support continue to be my greatest treasure. I am grateful to all the dancers who have kept singing games alive and to the Waldorf School movement for its enlightening perspectives on childhood. To the people, old and young, with whom I have learned and shared these dances, I sing my thanks. This book is a fruition of many years of collaboration with Lee Anne Welch, whose musical gifts grace my life. Thank you to Helen Caswell, also a lifelong family friend, whose drawings and paintings capture the essence of childhood. I send my deepest gratitude to Margret Meyerkort for her generous guidance. For technical expertise, thank you to John Eddy and Bill Kalogeros. Jim Peterson, Janet Kellman, Mia Michael, Margaret More, Liz Murray, and Polly Raven have contributed invaluable inspiration. My heartfelt thanks go to Nancy Mellon, editor and muse. To all these people and my students and their parents throughout the years, thank you for joining the dance!

From the Publisher
The Publisher would like to acknowledge Karl Franzen and Jerry Ashford for assistance with production of the CD included with this book and Lee Anne Welch for her perseverence and communication in facilitating its production.

Contents

Foreword

One rainy morning I visited Anna Rainville's public school and all the children were dancing. Teachers were singing and clapping. Even the most reluctant young people were studying the footwork and weaving the patterns of the line and partner dances she was calling. Anna stood on a table to direct the orchestra of movement activity. The dances rolled into one another and an indescribably determined and joyous spirit filled the hall. Shadows of early adolescent self-consciousness shrank into the corners of the room. Her confidence in the inherent truth and beauty of each dance had spread its contagion, and a mood of eager learning prevailed.

On another occasion when I was invited to give a talk to the parents at her California mountain school, Anna led singing games outdoors before the meeting. As the evening mists gathered in the trees, I was fascinated to see computer scientists and CEOs ducking and twining with artisans and harried working mothers, stepping the songs and dances that their children learned in the classroom. After a long day of work and striving, they so obviously loved being in the spell of the dance with Anna. The singing and movement surprised them. When it came time for my presentation on the art of storytelling, the spirit of the dance had opened their hearts and ears. The shared forms of spiral, circle and line brought them to innocent participation in life, which is the best starting point for any tale. The dances released a wellspring of community spirit.

At Anna's family home in Saratoga, California, not one of the seasonal celebrations in which I have been privileged to participate has begun without fiddle, song and dance. The live oaks and dancing green in their garden must await these special moments, when dozens of teachers, administrators, parents, community leaders and children gather to start the occasion with singing games. No matter that Anna had been cooking and organizing these events, at the key moment she leaps into the melée. Lee Anne plays the fiddle, and Anna begins to sing and call. Like swallows, in an instant everyone swirls into formation. Even the most tired teachers put down their tea and find their feet.

Over the years, Anna's singing games have rubbed off on countless people. I have sometimes overheard their grateful effusions as they report to her their growing ability to lead singing games in their own families, classrooms and communities. A home-schooling mother recently said, "Every day I apply what I have learned from Anna Rainville. I am so grateful to be able to share these singing games with my children and other families."

I highly recommend that you enjoy what Anna and Lee Anne have polished over so many years together. Seeds for this book were first cast as they capered and sashayed in Helen Caswell's festive front hall in winter, and on her spacious wooded lawn in summer when they were growing up together.

If you are a teacher and wish to invite the children you teach to find balance and gleeful kinesthetic skill, there can be no more enjoyable way to go about it. If you are a remedial specialist, there's much to be learned from the old wisdom weaving in these tunes and dance steps. If you are a family member who wishes to warm the core of joy hidden in daily struggles, choose a song in this book and take hands to find the buoyancy that has lifted generations. If you are baffled by community dynamics, look for a new and refreshing pattern in the pages of this book. Find your voice and put on your dusty dancing shoes. Here is a panacea that works!

Nancy Mellon
author of *Storytelling and the Art of Imagination*

Introduction

Gather together, in a circle we will sing. Gather together, we will make a golden ring.

Let the games begin! Singing games have strengthened the bodies and souls of Americans for generations. Recently I was reminded of this when I answered an invitation to contribute some singing games to a big family celebration. As the fiddler struck up "Bow Down, O Belinda," everyone, from the four-year-olds to the oldest grandparents, scrambled to find partners. I began to sing, and soon the catchy tune was sounded by all. "Right hands round... Left hands round." Then each group joined with another group. At last, we found ourselves standing in a huge circle, ready to dance on. The joy arose from everyone participating and moving together.

I am interested in reviving the singing game as a social art, as a means to build community whenever children and/or adults gather together. I have had the privilege and great pleasure of witnessing such gatherings many times on lawns, fields, in gymnasiums and schoolrooms, on beaches and in community halls. The playing of these games has a charming, harmonizing effect on groups of all ages. In this collection, you will find the singing games that have thus far been my favorites—in classrooms, backyards, living rooms, seasonal festivals, birthday parties, picnics, block parties, faculty meetings, teacher workshops, farewell parties, showers, memorial services, and conferences.

In these European-American singing games, you will find similarities to forms, themes, and melodies in singing games from many cultures. This book reflects my experience with the European-American singing game tradition. My cultural boundaries broaden every day in the classroom, and I look forward to publishing a more global collection when the time is ripe. I am grateful to those who continuously share with the children and me the singing games of their culture.

These games and their ancestors come from both noble and peasant stock. They have been danced by young and old in the fields, in the streets, and in great halls. People dancing and singing together are represented in clay and on canvas, in manuscripts and texts from ancient and contemporary cultures. The exact origins of some of these singing games are unknown; nevertheless, they have been kept alive by the children and their elders. They exist in many variations. The folk music tradition is always evolving and changing. In the cooperative spirit of the folk tradition, every effort has been made to identify the immediate lineage of each song.

Singing games allow the participants simultaneously to move and to sing together. Each of these activities is enlivening and empowering. When a group is gathered together, the combination of singing and dancing kindles an extraordinary and uplifting spirit of wholeness. It is this spirit that I wish to share with you.

THE VERY YOUNG

Very young children are made of sound and movement. Nothing is more contagious than the pleasure they find in their own childish voices and gestures. What is our adult role? It is to be a guiding presence, as we watch over them and provide a safe and caring atmosphere for them to explore movement, music, and song. Songs that can be repeated one thousand times or more in sing-song and repetition give them indescribable joy.

I find the melodies in the songs that follow soothing. The warmth and pure tones that sing through these songs are nourishment for children. They create a mood that brings me closer to the children in my care. Some of the songs are pentatonic. The five tones of the pentatonic scale can be played as do, re, fa, so, la. Any combination of these notes produces a perfect little melody, as in *Here We Go To Touch The Sky*. They create a mood akin to childhood. With these five tones, it is easy to make up little melodies for singing directions, expressing endearments, and enhancing verses and stories. As a teacher, I often sing or hum a song in the classroom as I am setting up an activity or when I am out in the playground. I want the children already to have heard the tune and words sung many times before we begin to dance. I encourage parents and teachers to find their singing voices, and to use them every day for the children's benefit.

Singing games for the very young call for the simplest of movements. With the youngest dancers, circling round together, raising arms, jumping, or sitting down at the end of the dance can be extremely satisfying.

As the youngest discover these movements together, they become for the first time a learning group. You will notice in these games that the children dance all together at the same time. As they grow, they will naturally stand more and more as individuals, and become increasingly more comfortable being alone in the middle of the circle. Until then, like a tender flock of ducklings, keep them under your sheltering wings.

When nursery school children and parents sing and dance these singing games together, some children will join hands, some will be carried, others ride piggy-back. All are invited to the dance! The participation of their dear elders in the singing games validates the children's own beginning experiences with movement. These first experiences will serve them well in developing coordination, concentration, and cooperation for the present and for the coming years.

Birthday Song

One, two, three, four, five, Five jour-neys 'round the sun.

Through the win-ter, spring, and sum-mer and fall, I

jour-ney 'round the sun. My new year has be-gun.

Melody and lyrics by Anna Rainville
This song was previously published in
Kindergarten Education by Betty Peck,
Hawthorn Press, Stroud, UK, 2005

I composed this birthday song for my mother, who wanted a new way to celebrate birthdays in her kindergarten class. On the day of the celebration, a small table representing the sun is decorated with candles and little vases, one for each year of the child's life. The child's classmates sit in a circle decorated with colored cloths to represent the rainbow trail that leads to earth. When the ceremony begins, everyone sings as the birthday child, wearing a cape and simple crown, holds the teacher's hand. Together they walk once around the sun-table.

1, 2, 3, 4, 5,
FIVE JOURNEYS 'ROUND THE SUN.
THROUGH THE WINTER, SPRING, AND SUMMER AND FALL,
I JOURNEY 'ROUND THE SUN.
MY NEW YEAR HAS BEGUN.

As it ends, the song pauses. An incident from the first year of the child's life is recounted. One candle is lit and one sprig is placed in a vase. I have prepared several days in advance by asking the parents about special incidents in their child's life. The child and teacher circle around again, singing for each year, always stopping as the song ends to tell about that year: a special trip, a favorite pet, a new friendship. When all the candles are lit, the child sits down at the table with a chosen friend, a guardian star-child. Then classmates come up, one by one, to wish the child Happy Birthday, give their hand-drawn cards, and receive a birthday treat. "Happy birthday, Sarah." "Thank you for the card. You may have a treat." "Thank you." To help gratitude ring out, the birthday parents and the teacher ring little bells every time a "thank you" sounds in the room.

The song can easily be adapted for six- or seven-year-olds. For a fifty-year old, we sang by tens: TEN, TWENTY, THIRTY, FORTY, FIFTY. After each decade, ten little tea lights were lit and stories told. Needless to say, the table was ablaze with light at the end of the journey.

Ceremonial dance
All ages

Fiddle Me Up

English

Young children are made of pure music. They move and dance spontaneously. Here is an example of a tune that travels up and down the five-tone pentatonic scale. See the children's joy as they tune their bodies to the melody in this simple dance. The youngest children begin by standing in a circle to sing.

FIDDLE ME UP TO LONDON TOWN.
FIDDLE ME DOWN TO DOVER.
I'LL DANCE WHILE THE MUSIC PLAYS,
The children mime a fiddler playing the violin with a lively bow.

AND I'LL STOP WHEN IT'S OVER.
On OVER the children "freeze." Then they take up another instrument, such as a drum, a guitar or a flute, and continue the song.

DRUM ME UP...
STRUM ME UP...
TOOT ME UP...

A variation for children seven and older is to follow the leader in a line around the room or the garden while singing the song and miming.

Circle or line game
Age 5 and older

Singing Games

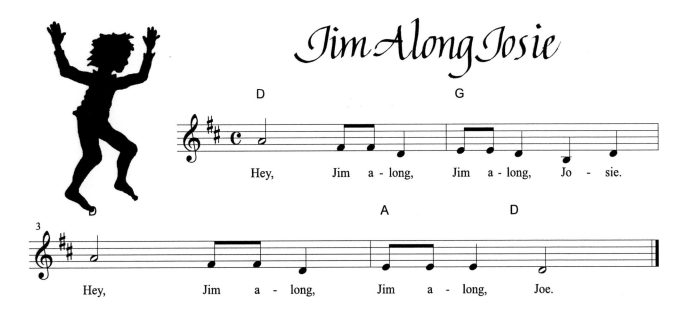

Jim Along Josie

Hey, Jim a - long, Jim a - long, Jo - sie.

Hey, Jim a - long, Jim a - long, Joe.

American

All children require movement in order to awaken and integrate their many intelligences. It is a joy for both teachers and children to ease into lessons with kinesthetic exercise. To begin this singing game, the teacher stands with the children in a circle singing:

**HEY, JIM ALONG,
JIM ALONG, JOSIE.
HEY, JIM ALONG,
JIM ALONG, JOE.**
The children stand in a circle and circle to the left as they sing this first verse.

**WALK, JIM ALONG,
JIM ALONG, JOSIE.
WALK, JIM ALONG,
JIM ALONG, JOE.**
The children follow the action suggested by the words of the song.

Additional verses include skipping, hopping, crawling, rocking, walking backward, hopping and so on. This song can be adapted for therapeutic movement, such as cross crawling and improving their sense of balance. Older children enjoy following the leader as they sing and gesture appropriately in a line.

Circle or line dance
Age 5 and older

The Very Young

Here We Go 'Round the Mulberry Bush

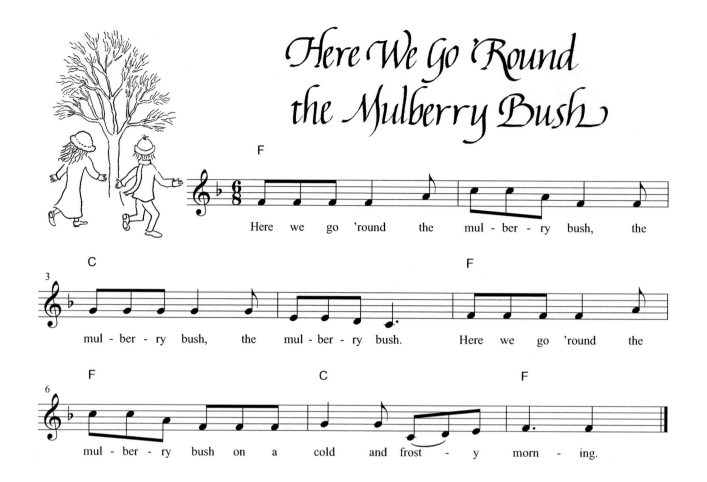

Here we go 'round the mul - ber - ry bush, the mul - ber - ry bush, the mul - ber - ry bush. Here we go 'round the mul - ber - ry bush on a cold and frost - y morn - ing.

English

Singing games set healthy rhythms in motion. Households of not so long ago maintained reassuring weekly routines. This old English singing game, like children's songs throughout the world, presents a pattern for healthy housekeeping and sensible living. Some versions of this song specify a customary day of the week for each chore: Mondays for washing, Tuesdays for ironing, Wednesdays for mending, and so on. Although our pace of life has accelerated, the need for healthy rhythm in children's lives has not changed. To begin this singing game, the children stand in a circle holding hands. Everyone sings:

Chorus:
**HERE WE GO 'ROUND THE MULBERRY BUSH,
THE MULBERRY BUSH, THE MULBERRY BUSH.
HERE WE GO 'ROUND THE MULBERRY BUSH
ON A COLD AND FROSTY MORNING.**
The children circle to the left during these lines of the chorus. As the other verses are sung, they stand in place and mime the action described in the verse.

THIS IS THE WAY WE WASH OUR CLOTHES...

THIS IS THE WAY WE IRON OUR CLOTHES...

THIS IS THE WAY WE MEND OUR CLOTHES...

THIS IS THE WAY WE SWEEP OUR FLOORS...

THIS IS THE WAY WE SCRUB OUR FLOORS...

The mulberry, with its delicious sweet berries, is a common feature in English gardens.

This song can be adapted to teach children about personal hygiene.
THIS IS THE WAY WE BRUSH OUR TEETH. THIS IS THE WAY WE WASH OUR FACE. THIS IS THE WAY WE BRUSH OUR HAIR...

English
Circle game
Age 4 and older

Here We Go to Touch the Sky

Here we go to touch the sky.

G

Now we go to touch the earth. Low, high, low, high.

Melody and lyrics by Beth Everette

The role of the adult in children's lives is to help them feel at home upon the earth and to discover the world around them with gratitude. Beth Everette, a devoted gardener and musician, wrote this song for my mother's kindergarten. The wise openness of the ascending and descending five-tone pentatonic scale speaks in a language familiar and reassuring to the young child. To begin, the children may be seated or standing.

HERE WE GO TO TOUCH THE SKY.
The children reach up slowly with their arms toward the sky.

NOW WE GO TO TOUCH THE EARTH.
The children lower their arms slowly and touch the floor.

LOW, HIGH,
LOW, HIGH.
They repeat these gestures.

A variation for this simple yet powerful song is for the children to raise their fingers… arms…elbows…legs…heads up and down as they sing.

Circle play
Age 3 and older

Singing Games

Nix in the Water

Nix in the wa - ter, you are the ri - ver king's

daugh - ter. Wash your legs with sil - ver sand and

tie your hair with a gol - den band. Nix catch me.

Melody by Jennifer Aulie, lyrics by Margret Meyerkort
Used with the kind permission of Wynstones Press

A "nix" or "nixie" is a water sprite. Children love to pretend they are playful elementals.
This simple five-tone pentatonic song tickles their senses and sparks imagination. To be-
gin, the children stand in a circle. Everyone sings:

NIX IN THE WATER,
YOU ARE THE RIVER KING'S DAUGHTER.
Several children are chosen to be nixes and sit in the middle.

WASH YOUR LEGS WITH SILVER SAND
All the children mime washing their legs with silver sand.

AND TIE YOUR HAIR WITH A GOLDEN BAND.
All the children mime tying up their hair with a golden band.

NIX CATCH ME.
The nixes jump up and choose a child from the circle by putting their arms around them.
The chosen ones are the new nixes and the game continues.

Circle game
Age 5 and older

See the Little Hare

See the lit-tle hare so fast a - sleep, fast a - sleep. Lit - tle hare, oh are you ill, that you lie so qui-et and still? Hop, lit-tle hare, Hop, lit-tle hare, hop a - ny - where.

German

Rabbits prefer company and live in warrens, and hares are solitary creatures that rise up on their hind legs and look out to the distant horizon. In this song, the little hare proves to be alert and capable of infinite activity. To begin, the young dancers stand in a circle. Everyone sings:

SEE THE LITTLE HARE SO FAST ASLEEP, FAST ASLEEP.
LITTLE HARE, OH ARE YOU ILL,
THAT YOU LIE SO QUIET AND STILL?

One or more children are chosen to be little hares and sit very quietly in the middle of the circle.

HOP, LITTLE HARE,
HOP, LITTLE HARE,
HOP ANYWHERE.

Each hare hops in front of a child standing in the circle and places his or her hands on the chosen one's shoes. Those children are now the new hares.

This game is helpful for young children who don't want to make direct eye contact when choosing.

For the very youngest dancers, everyone can play at being hares, resting quietly on the first three lines, and hopping about on the last line.

Open circle or circle dance
Age 3 and older

Sally Go 'Round the Sun

F

Sal - ly go 'round the sun. Sal - ly go 'round the

F   C   F

moon. Sal - ly go 'round the chim - ney pots on a Sat - ur - day af - ter - noon. Woops!

English

ALTERNATE MELODY

Sal - ly go 'round the sun. Sal - ly go 'round the moon.

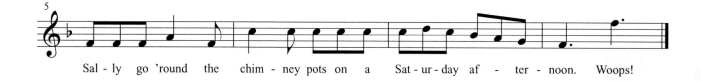

Sal - ly go 'round the chim - ney pots on a Sat - ur - day af - ter - noon. Woops!

The simplest song can touch the deepest mysteries. It is no wonder that children find this singing story so endlessly satisfying as they re-enact the journey from their celestial origins to their earthly home and hearth. "Sally" is a variant of "Sarah," which means "princess." Every child has the royal task of becoming a wise ruler on the earth. This singing game can be easily adapted to different age groups. To begin, ask the very youngest children to join hands in a golden sun-circle.

Variation One

SALLY GO 'ROUND THE SUN.
SALLY GO 'ROUND THE MOON.
SALLY GO 'ROUND THE CHIMNEY POTS
ON A SATURDAY AFTERNOON.

All the children circle to the left.

WOOPS!

The children stop and raise arms up, and then lower them again.

Variation Two

SALLY GO 'ROUND THE SUN.
SALLY GO 'ROUND THE MOON.

Five- and six-year-old children join hands and circle to the left.

SALLY GO 'ROUND THE CHIMNEY POTS

The children drop hands and turn around in place.

ON A SATURDAY AFTERNOON.

The children join hands again

WOOPS!

and raise their arms up and down again, as they take a step in toward the center.

Variation Three

SALLY GO 'ROUND THE SUN.

Six- and seven-year-old children join hands and circle left.

SALLY GO 'ROUND THE MOON.

Everyone circles right.

SALLY GO 'ROUND THE CHIMNEY POTS

They drop hands and turn around in place.

ON A SATURDAY AFTERNOON.

Everyone joins hands again and steps toward the center of the circle

WOOPS

—and all raise their arms up and down again.

Circle dance
Age 4 and older

Ring Around the Rosie

Ring a - round the ros - ie. Pock - et full of po - sies.

Ash - es, ash - es we all fall down.

English

ALTERNATE MELODY AND WORDS

Ring a ring o' ro - ses, A pock - et full of po - sies, a

tish - oo a tish - oo. All fall down.

Singing Games

Every now and then someone might startle you by saying that this favorite rhyme has something to do with the devastating Great Plague in England in 1665. It does not. Please refer to the Opies' scholarly work The Singing Game *to settle any rumor. There are other ways of looking at the meaning of the rhyme. Margret Meyerkort, who penetrated the secrets of singing games over many years as a teacher of young children, offers an allegorical interpretation. The ring is a symbol of eternity. The rose in its essential structure of a five-pointed star, is a picture of the human soul. Sneezes are awakening. And in the tradition of the old rhymes, such as "Rock-a-bye baby," "Goosey goosey gander" and "Humpty Dumpty," falling down is a picture of incarnating. Ring Around the Rosie pictures the spirit child circling before descending into an earthly birth. To begin dancing to this old rhyme, everyone joins hands in a circle and sings:*

RING AROUND THE ROSIE.
POCKET FULL OF POSIES.
A-TISHOO, A-TISHOO (or ASHES, ASHES)
Everyone circles left.
WE ALL FALL DOWN.
Everyone squats or falls down.

This is the simplest of games and immensely satisfying to the youngest dancer. It is worth indulging your young one's request to play it over and over again.   Often one might hear the original version accompanied by a verse to get the children up again. These words were added in the 1950s, to help the children return to order after rolling on the floor!

COWS IN THE MEADOW
EATING BUTTERCUPS
A-TISHOO, A-TISHOO
Children remain squatting.
WE ALL JUMP UP!
Everyone jumps up to begin circling again.

A-TISHOO OVER THE OCEAN
A-TISHOO OVER THE SEA
A-TISHOO OVER THE CHIMNEY POT
Children remain squatting.
AND UP JUMP WE!
Everyone jumps up to begin circling again.

Circle game
All ages

Rosy Apple

C   F C   G7

Ros - y ap - ple, mel - low pear, bunch of ros - es she shall wear,

C   F   C   G7   C

gold and sil - ver by her side, I know who shall be my bride.

English

Singing games endure partly due to their pure simplicity. This traditional English song distills love to a sweet essence. It has been called by Iona and Peter Opie in their definitive text, The Singing Game, *"one of the loveliest songs for 'playing ring' that ever haunted a city back street." Martin Shaw said he "would have given all his musical compositions to have composed it." To enjoy* Rosy Apple *as a dance, begin by forming a circle, along with generations of children, and join hands. Everyone sings:*

> **ROSY APPLE, MELLOW PEAR,**
> **BUNCH OF ROSES SHE SHALL WEAR,**
> **GOLD AND SILVER BY HER SIDE,**
> **I KNOW WHO SHALL BE MY BRIDE.**

For young children, the circle moves to the left as two to four bridegrooms are chosen to stand in the middle.

> **TAKE HER BY HER LILY-WHITE HAND;**
> **LEAD HER 'CROSS THE WATER;**
> **GIVE HER KISSES ONE, TWO, THREE;**
> **SHE'S A LADY'S DAUGHTER.**

The dancers stand still and raise their arms to form arches. The bridegrooms choose brides from the circle and move in and out of the arches.

A variation for the second verse is for the bridegrooms to lead their brides through only one arch and then return to the center of the circle for the last two bars. The bridegrooms then join the circle as the brides become the new bridegrooms, and the game begins again.

Circle game
Age 6 and older

Who'll Come into My Wee Ring

Who-'ll come in - to my wee ring, my wee ring, my wee ring?

Who-'ll come in - to my wee ring, and make it a wee bit big - ger?

English

This cozy song is a comforting way to form a circle. Young children feel safe in its embrace. To begin, the children are seated on the floor as the teacher takes one child by the hand and sings:

> **WHO'LL COME INTO MY WEE RING,**
> **MY WEE RING, MY WEE RING?**
> **WHO'LL COME INTO MY WEE RING,**
> **AND MAKE IT A WEE BIT BIGGER?**

They walk around together.

> **(Name of child or children) WILL COME INTO MY WEE RING,**
> **MY WEE RING, MY WEE RING.**
> **(Name) WILL COME INTO MY WEE RING,**
> **AND MAKE IT A WEE BIT BIGGER.**

The teacher calls to another child who is sitting or standing close by to join in. The song continues until all the children are included, and a circle has been formed.

For children of six and older, the leader stands in the middle of the circle and sings the question. As the second verse begins, a child is chosen to sing the response I'LL COME INTO YOUR WEE RING... The child joins the growing inner circle and the game continues.

Circle game
Age 3 and older

Gallant Ship

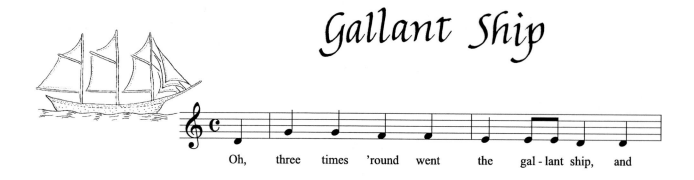

Oh, three times 'round went the gal - lant ship, and

three times 'round went she. And three times 'round went the gal - lant ship, as she

sank to the bot - tom of the sea, as she sank to the bot - tom of the sea.

English

ALTERNATE MELODY

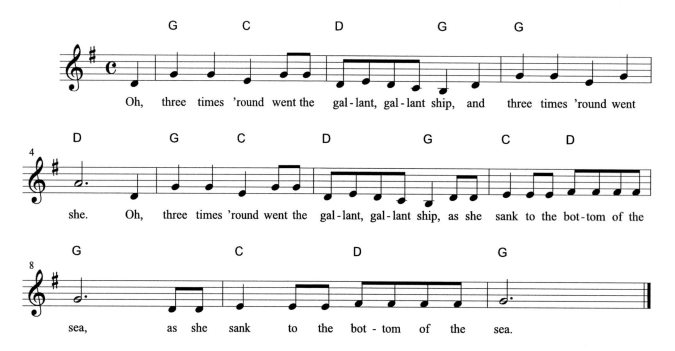

Oh, three times 'round went the gal - lant, gal - lant ship, and three times 'round went

she. Oh, three times 'round went the gal - lant, gal - lant ship, as she sank to the bot - tom of the

sea, as she sank to the bot - tom of the sea.

Children revel in discovering their own resilience. They love and need to explore all the directions: forward, backward, right, left, up, and down. In this nautical tune from maritime Britain, the children can experience a resounding levity and gravity. To begin, the children join hands in a circle. Everyone sings:

OH, THREE TIMES 'ROUND WENT THE GALLANT SHIP,
AND THREE TIMES 'ROUND WENT SHE.
AND THREE TIMES 'ROUND WENT THE GALLANT SHIP,
The children circle left.

AS SHE SANK TO THE BOTTOM OF THE SEA,
AS SHE SANK TO THE BOTTOM OF THE SEA.
The children gradually sink to the ground.

"PULL HER UP, PULL HER UP," CRIED THE JOLLY SAILOR BOY.
"PULL HER UP, PULL HER UP," CRIED HE.
"PULL HER UP, PULL HER UP," CRIED THE JOLLY SAILOR BOY,
"'TIL SHE COMES TO THE TOP OF THE SEA,"
"'TIL SHE COMES TO THE TOP OF THE SEA."
The children gradually rise up again.

Variation:
"PULL HER UP..."
'ERE SHE SINKS TO THE BOTTOM OF THE SEA."
The children circle left and sink down on the last line.

Circle dance
Age 4 and older

OCCUPATIONS

Whenever I am teaching adults to lead the singing games that follow, I always say, "Make sure your gestures are worthy of imitation. As we all know, children will imitate our every twitch!" The gestures and miming in these games are simple and deliberate. Verisimilitude is important. If the song calls for shoveling, mime holding the shovel accurately for planting, as in *Old Roger*. If the song calls for washing, as in *The Washerwomen*, mime wringing out wet clothes with the traditional figure-eight, lemniscate motion. Authentically broadcast seed in a clockwise motion, as in *The Farmer In The Dell*.

Even though the occupations described in the songs that follow may seem old-fashioned, they hold ennobling pictures of good work being well done. For hundreds of years these singing games have helped prepare children for useful work.

OCCUPATIONS

Blow, Wind, Blow

Blow, wind, blow, and go, mill, go, That the mil - ler may grind his corn, That the ba - ker may take it and in - to bread bake it, and bring us a loaf in the morn, and bring us a loaf in the morn.

Mother Goose rhyme, Slovak folk melody

Singing Games

This song is a way to dance the story of wheat being ground at the mill, a motif that appears often in middle-European folk and fairy tales. One child is chosen to be the winged arms of the mill, and stands in the middle on a low stool or wooden block. Several children make a small circle holding hands around the mill. They are the grinding stone. The rest of the children are the wind and stand in a circle around the stone without holding hands. The wind begins by stepping forward and back, rocking in place. Then the wind-children push their arms forward and back, making a gentle whooshing, windy sound. When the wind has begun to blow, the wings of the mill turn and the child who is the mill rotates outstretched arms. Finally, when the mill is in motion, the stone begins to move. It circles to the left as everyone sings:

BLOW, WIND, BLOW,
AND GO, MILL, GO,
THAT THE MILLER MAY GRIND HIS CORN,*
THAT THE BAKER MAY TAKE IT AND INTO BREAD BAKE IT,
AND BRING US A LOAF IN THE MORN,
AND BRING US A LOAF IN THE MORN.

This is a very rhythmical piece and soothing to the children. Visiting adults enjoy being a tall mill.

*Throughout the United Kingdom, wheat is referred to as corn.

Especially appropriate for autumn harvest themes and bread baking
Circle dance
Age 6 and older

The Farmer in the Dell

The far-mer in the dell, the farm-er in the dell.

Hi - ho the der - ry - o, the far - mer in the dell.

Adapted from the English

In the autumn I tell the old English fairy tale of The Little Red Hen, who one morning while scratching in the barnyard finds a wheat seed. The story recounts her industrious independence that eventually results in a warm loaf of bread. In the classroom we bake our own bread, accompanied by this version of the old familiar song and dance.

THE FARMER IN THE DELL, THE FARMER IN THE DELL.
HI-HO THE DERRY-O, THE FARMER IN THE DELL.
The children join hands and circle to the left.

THE FARMER SOWS THE SEED...
The children mime sowing wheat seed from a sack over their shoulders.

THE WIND BEGINS TO BLOW...
The children mime the blowing wind.

THE RAINS BEGIN TO FALL...
They mime the falling rain.

THE SUN BEGINS TO SHINE...
They mime the shining sun by reaching up with their arms and encircling their heads.

THE WHEAT BEGINS TO GROW...
They crouch down and slowly grow up, reaching their arms toward the sky.

A variation on the above is to choose several children to curl up in the center of the circle to be the newly sown wheat seeds. Other children can be chosen to be the wind, the rain, and the sun. Simple colored capes or cloths can add to the drama. The story of the wheat may continue over the course of several days with the following verses:

THE FARMER CUTS THE WHEAT...
An adult comes around and runs a finger lightly across the child's tummy to mime the harvesting of the wheat. Each wheat stalk-child then falls to the ground. I explain that in order for the stalks to dry, they must lie without touching one another.

THE SUN DRIES THE WHEAT...
THE FARMER BUNDLES THE WHEAT...
THE FARMER THRESHES THE WHEAT...
THE FARMER WINNOWS THE WHEAT...
THE FARMER GOES TO THE MILL...
THE MILLER GRINDS THE WHEAT...
THE FARMER GOES TO THE BAKER...
THE BAKER BAKES THE BREAD...
THE BAKER KNEADS THE DOUGH...
THE BREAD BEGINS TO RISE...
THE CHILDREN EAT THE BREAD...

If you are creating a circle time for young children in the autumn, include this singing game with other verses and songs about farmers and harvest, such as *Blow, Wind, Blow*. Let *The Farmer in the Dell* tune inspire other verses about mills, wind, or grinding to add between the traditional verses.

Bread-making activities add to the joy and meaning of the dance
Age 5 and older

John Kanaka

Verse

I thought I heard the old man say,

John Ka - na - ka, na - ka, too - la - ay. To -

day, to - day is a sail - ing day.

John Ka - na - ka, na - ka, too - la - ay.

Refrain

Too - la - ay, oh too - la - ay.

John Ka - na - ka, na - ka, too - la - ay.

Sea chantey

Never doubt the salutary benefits of well-organized stamping and clapping. This sea chantey contains a term "kanaka," referring to the Hawaiian sailor. The rolling gait of the song helps the children learn to embody the power of the ocean's roll. It calls out gusto in even the mildest little sailor. To begin, the children stand in a circle.

Verse:

I THOUGHT I HEARD THE OLD MAN SAY,
The children in the circle sing.

JOHN KANAKA, NAKA, TOO-LA-AY.
The children stamp their feet, slap their knees twice, clap their hands twice and hold both palms out toward the center of the circle.

TODAY, TODAY IS A SAILING DAY.
The children stand and sing.

JOHN KANAKA, NAKA, TOO-LA-AY.
The children stamp their feet, slap their knees twice, clap their hands twice and hold both palms out toward the center of the circle.

Refrain:
TOO LA AY OH TOO-LA-AY.
The children turn around once in place.

JOHN KANAKA, NAKA, TOO-LA-AY.
The children stamp their feet, slap their knees twice, clap their hands twice and hold both palms out toward the center of the circle.

Verse:
WE'RE OUTWARD BOUND FROM 'FRISCO BAY.
JOHN KANAKA, NAKA, TOO-LA-AY.
WE'RE OUTWARD BOUND AT BREAK OF DAY.
JOHN KANAKA, NAKA, TOO-LA-AY...
Repeat gestures, as above.

Refrain

Verse:
IT'S WEEVILY MEAT AND MOLDY BREAD...
IT'S TWO MONTHS OUT, YOU'D WISH YOU'RE DEAD...

Refrain

A variation is for the children to stand in two concentric circles. Each faces a partner in the other circle. When the words JOHN KANAKA NAKA are sung, as above, they stamp their feet, slap their knees twice, clap their hands twice. In this version, on the AY of TOO-LA-AY, they clap both hands with their partners. On the refrain, the inside circle remains stationary, as the outside circle travels left one place to stand before their new partners, ready to sing the next verse of the song. Other variations for the refrain include do-si-do-ing (walking once around back-to-back with a partner) or taking hands with a partner and turning once around.

Circle dance
Ages 8 and older

Oats, Peas, Beans and Barley Grow

Oats, peas, beans and bar-ley grow. Oats, peas, beans and bar-ley grow. Do you or I or an-y-one know, how oats, peas, beans and bar-ley grow?

English

ALTERNATE MELODY

Oats, peas, beans and bar-ley grow. Oats, peas, beans and bar-ley grow. Do
First the farm-er sows his seeds, then he stops and takes his ease. He

you or I or an-y-one know how oats, peas, beans and bar-ley grow?
stamps his foot, he claps his hand and then he turns to view his land.

Wait-ing for a part-ner, wait-ing for a part-ner, o-pen the door and let one in.

Now you're mar-ried you must o-bey. You must be true to all you say. You

must be kind, you must be good, and help your wife to chop the wood.

Singing Games

Farmers and gardeners, the caretakers of the earth, are unsung heroes. It is never too early or too late for children to connect with the realities of their daily food. In this beloved English singing game, the work of the farmer is celebrated. To begin, the children stand in a circle with joined hands. Everyone sings:

OATS, PEAS, BEANS AND BARLEY GROW.
OATS, PEAS, BEANS AND BARLEY GROW.
DO YOU OR I OR ANYONE KNOW,
HOW OATS, PEAS, BEANS AND BARLEY GROW?
The children circle to the left.

Additional verses for the first melody:

FIRST THE FARMER SOWS HIS SEED,
The children stop to mime sowing.

THEN HE STANDS AND TAKES HIS EASE
Children stand still and visibly relax…

HE STAMPS HIS FOOT AND CLAPS HIS HAND
…stamp their feet and clap their hands…

AND TURNS AROUND TO VIEW THE LAND.
and turn around with their hand shading their eyes as if looking out across their fields.

WAITING FOR A PARTNER,
WAITING FOR A PARTNER,
OPEN THE RING AND TAKE ONE IN
WHILE WE ALL GAILY DANCE AND SING.
The children turn to their neighbors, take hands, and dance together.

NOW YOU'RE MARRIED YOU MUST OBEY.
YOU MUST BE TRUE TO ALL YOU SAY.
YOU MUST BE KIND, YOU MUST BE GOOD,
AND HELP YOUR WIFE TO CHOP THE WOOD.
The children circle left. They stop and mime chopping wood on the last line.

For young children, the parent or teacher can stand in the middle of the circle with one of the children who has been chosen to be the farmer. With older children, choose one or two farmers to stand in the middle of the circle and act out the verses. On the second verse, the farmers choose partners from the circle and all dance in the middle. On the last verse, the farmers and their wives join hands and circle right as the outer circle moves to the left.

Circle game
Age 6 and older

Pop Goes the Weasel

D   A   D   A

All a-round the cob-bler's bench, The mon-key chased the

D   A   D   G A

wea-sel. That's the way the mon-ey goes. Pop! goes the

D   G   A   E7

wea-sel. A pen-ny for a spool of thread. A pen-ny for a

A   G   A   D

nee-dle. That's the way the mon-ey goes. Pop! goes the wea-sel.

English

A steady working rhythm is a song in itself. It is easy to understand why work songs have arisen around most professions. The "weasel" in this song refers to a sewing tool used by cobblers, tailors and hatters. When its spool was full it "popped," a sound that punctuated the lives of these working families. To begin, everyone joins hands in groups of three, and circles left.

**ALL AROUND THE COBBLER'S BENCH,
THE MONKEY CHASED THE WEASEL.
THAT'S THE WAY THE MONEY GOES.
POP! GOES THE WEASEL.**

**A PENNY FOR A SPOOL OF THREAD.
A PENNY FOR A NEEDLE.
THAT'S THE WAY THE MONEY GOES.
POP! GOES THE WEASEL.**

On the word POP, one child – the weasel – still holding hands with the others, stoops under the arch formed by the other two. The weasel then returns back to place, as everyone continues to circle and sing the next verse. The children take turns being the weasel and popping under. Once everyone is familiar with the game, all the players who "pop" slip under the arches and scurry off to complete a neighboring circle of three. This can cause a chaotic rush of weasels, seeking new circles. A more orderly procedure can be established by directing each weasel to travel clockwise from circle to circle on the word POP.

Circle game
Age 6 and older.

Occupations

Shepherd Maiden

See a shep-herd mai-den here,   stand-ing with her   sheep so near.

With   a   part - ner   she   will   make   for   the   sheep   a   lit - tle   gate.

1. Run - ning   quick - ly   they   will   pass,   To   the   up - land   mea - dow   grass,
2. Shep herd   mai - den,   call   them home.   Day   is   done, no   more   to   roam.

Where   the   pas - ture   is   the   best,   'Til   the   sun   sets   in   the   west.
Safe   with - in   the   guard - ed   fold,   Shel - ter   them from   harm   and   cold.

French

The melodic French tune of this dance invites the children into a gentle pastoral mood. They love to act out the archetypal journey of going out into the world and returning safely home. To begin the dance, a small family of sheep children with their mother nestle inside a circle of standing children who are holding hands to represent the sheepfold. A child is chosen to be the ewe and another one to be the shepherd or shepherdess. Everyone sings:

SEE A SHEPHERD MAIDEN (BOY) HERE,
STANDING WITH HER (HIS) SHEEP SO NEAR.
WITH A PARTNER SHE (HE) WILL MAKE
FOR THE SHEEP A LITTLE GATE.

The shepherd child makes an arch with the neighbor child as they both hold hands.

RUNNING QUICKLY THEY WILL PASS,
TO THE UPLAND MEADOW GRASS,
WHERE THE PASTURE IS THE BEST,
'TIL THE SUN SETS IN THE WEST.

The sheep venture under the arch and follow their mother to graze in a designated place in the room.

SHEPHERD MAIDEN, CALL THEM HOME.
DAY IS DONE, NO MORE TO ROAM.

The shepherd child gestures for the sheep to return. They follow their mother back through the gate and nestle in the middle of the sheepfold.

SAFE WITHIN THE GUARDED FOLD,
SHELTER THEM FROM HARM AND COLD.

The circle of children and the shepherd stretch out their arms to the center of the circle to form a little cozy roof for the sleeping sheep.

Circle dance
Age 5 and older

Shepherd's Hey

D G D A D G A D

I can whis-tle, I can sing, I can do most an-y-thing!

D G D A D G A D

I can dance and I can play, I can do the shep-herd's hey. La

D G D A D G A D

la la la la la la la la la la la la la la la la la.

English

This traditional Morris Dance* has been enjoyed in England for centuries. Each spring teams of Morris Dancers visit the newly planted fields to wake up the grain with their vigorous, sprightly leaping steps and accompanying music. To add to the sense of returning life, the dancers wear bells sewn on ribbons tied just below their knees. Children easily catch the joyous spirit of the tune and steps. To begin, the dancers assemble in a circle or line. Everyone sings:

I CAN WHISTLE, I CAN SING,
The dancers take seven steps in place.

I CAN DO MOST ANYTHING!
They clap seven times.

I CAN DANCE AND I CAN PLAY,
They take seven steps in place and stop.

I CAN DO THE SHEPHERD'S HEY.
They clap seven times.

LA LA LA LA

The dancers clap twice and gesture to the right.

LA LA LA LA

They clap twice and gesture to the left.

LA LA LA LA LA LA LA

The dancers clap and then lift one leg and clap under it.
They repeat this pattern with the other leg.

LA LA LA

They clap in front, clap in back, and clap in front.

As the children become more skillful, it is delightful to experiment with different gestures for the LA LAs. The only rule is that after the two claps, whatever is performed on one side must then be repeated on the other side. For example, if the dancers touch their heels in back with their right hands, then they must touch their heels in back with their left hands.

To vary the dance, instead of standing in place, take seven steps forward. Clap seven times and then take seven steps backwards and clap seven times. Changing the tempo is also exciting. Start out at a moderate tempo. Gradually with each verse speed up until you are going like wildfire! Then end the dance with a very slow rendition. All the steps of this dance can also be accomplished in a crowded classroom, as the children stand behind their desks.

* See Resources

Circle or line dance
Age 7 and older

The Blacksmith

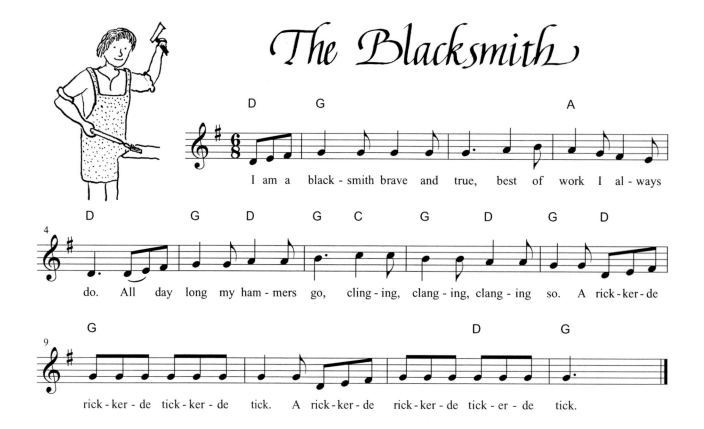

I am a black-smith brave and true, best of work I al-ways do. All day long my ham-mers go, cling-ing, clang-ing, clang-ing so. A rick-ker-de rick-ker-de tick-ker-de tick. A rick-ker-de rick-ker-de tick-er-de tick.

Dutch

This lively game with lots of strong, willful gestures is originally from Holland. Although the blacksmith is not a familiar sight for most American children today, the image of a strong man standing by his fiery forge to accomplish his daily tasks is an intriguing one to bring to children. During this dance, a circle form is not necessary, as each child stands independently in a separate space. The song begins with the children pointing proudly to themselves.

I AM A BLACKSMITH BRAVE AND TRUE,
BEST OF WORK I ALWAYS DO.
The children place their hands in front of them with their palms up.

ALL DAY LONG MY HAMMERS GO,
CLINGING, CLANGING, CLANGING SO.
The children make hammer gestures alternating with their left and right fists.

A RIKKERDE RIKKERDE TIKKERDE TICK.
A RIKKERDE RIKKERDE TIKKERDE TICK.
On the first time through, the children mime hammering with the closed fist of their right hands.

On the second time through the song the children mime hammering with both fists at the same time.

The dance continues with chorus and verses, each time adding another hammer. On the third time, they mime hammering with both hands and one foot; the fourth time, with both hands and both feet. On the last time, they mime with both hands, both feet and head!

Individual dance
Age 5 and older

See Mother's a-Weaving

See mo-ther's a-weav-ing up-on the big loom, and the

shut-tle, yes, the shut-tle, it goes to and fro. Like the

shut-tle, yes, the shut-tle, we dance to and fro.

Norwegian

This singing game provides a musical experience of the craft of weaving. Children love to enter their parents' work through play. Hands creating beautiful necessities out of soft fibers on wooden looms that are creaking to a reassuring rhythm offer a very different ambience from that of the instantaneous clicking of electronic inventions. The present resurgence in handcrafts, such as knitting, spinning, and weaving, bodes well for our children's future. To begin, children gather in groups of four.

SEE MOTHER'S A-WEAVING UPON THE BIG LOOM,
The foursome claps their hands four times to the beat of the music.

AND THE SHUTTLE, YES, THE SHUTTLE,
IT GOES TO AND FRO.
LIKE THE SHUTTLE, YES, THE SHUTTLE,
WE DANCE TO AND FRO.
Two children stand facing each other and reach across to join hands. The other two in each group of four do the same, placing their joined hands on top of the first couple's hands. Now placing one foot slightly forward and the other back for balance, everyone rocks gently forward and backward, seesawing in place.

A circle game for groups of four
Age 7 and older

The Thread Follows the Needle

The thread fol-lows the nee-dle. The thread fol-lows the nee-dle. 'Round and 'round the nee-dle goes. That's the way we mend our clothes.

American

As children learn to attend to fine details in their immediate surroundings, they gradually discover how essential little parts are to the whole. A pointed little needle and a long firm thread can provide endless satisfaction, as children learn to sew up their own creations and to mend. When adults sit down to sew, their patient rhythmic stitches are teaching children more than meets the eye. During the winter circle in the kindergarten, we sing this song and pretend we are mending a woodcutter's jacket that was torn when he was chopping wood for the fire. This American singing game resembles similar "thread the needle" dances from other lands. To begin, children hold hands in a line and sing:

THE THREAD FOLLOWS THE NEEDLE.
THE THREAD FOLLOWS THE NEEDLE.
'ROUND AND 'ROUND THE NEEDLE GOES.
THAT'S THE WAY WE MEND OUR CLOTHES.

The first child in line is called "the Thread." The child at the opposite end of the line is called "the Needle." The Needle pulls the line under the arch made by the Thread and his neighbor. When all the line has passed under the arch, the Thread, still holding hands with the line, is turned. This child now discovers her arms are crossed in front of her, like a little stitch. The next child in line, who is standing beside the first little stitch, will become the next stitch as the Needle continues to pull the line under the next arch. The Needle continues until everyone is neatly stitched. Repeat the song as many times as necessary to accomplish this. At the end of the game, ask a little mouse to come and nibble each stitch loose, so that the game can start again.

Line game
Age 6 and older

Occupations

Nana, Thread Needle

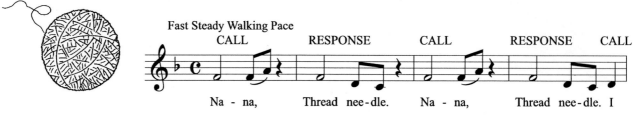

Fast Steady Walking Pace

CALL   RESPONSE   CALL   RESPONSE   CALL

Na - na,   Thread nee - dle.   Na - na,   Thread nee - dle. I

RESPONSE   CALL   RESPONSE   CALL

wants my nee - dle.   Thread nee - dle. I lost my nee - dle.   Thread nee - dle. My

Repeat ad lib until dance figure is complete.

RESPONSE   CALL   RESPONSE

gold - eyed nee - dle.   Thread nee - dle. It's ma - ma's nee - dle.   Thread nee - dle.

Briskly   EVERYONE

1. Going to wind up - a this bun - kum, bun - kum, Wind up - a this bun - kum.
2. Going to shake down - a this bun - kum, bun - kum, shake down - a this bun - kum.
3. Going to un - wind - a this bun - kum, bun - kum, un - wind - a this bun - kum.

wind up - a this bun - kum, bun - kum, Wind up - a this bun - kum.
shake down - a this bun - kum, bun - kum, shake down - a this bun - kum.
un - wind - a this bun - kum, bun - kum, un - wind - a this bun - kum.

Nana Thread Needle, new words and new music adaptations by Bessie Jones
Collected and edited by Alan Lomax

This lively variation of Thread the Needle is still enjoyed by the children of the Georgia Sea Islands, off the coast of North Carolina. It was collected by folk artist Bessie Jones, author of the classic Step It Down: Games, Plays, Songs and Stories from the Afro-American Heritage. *"Nana" in this four-part singing play, means "Mama." The first verse is a sung "call and response" dialogue between a caller and the other dancers. This part can stand alone as a singing game. To begin, the dancers join hands and form a line. Bessie Jones arranges her dancers according to height, from the shortest to the tallest. The dancers hold their joined hands up making a row of arches. The caller can be the tallest or any strong singer in the group. The caller stands at the head of the line and begins to sing:*

Caller:	NANA,	Dancers:	THREAD NEEDLE.
	NANA,		THREAD NEEDLE.
	I WANTS MY NEEDLE.		THREAD NEEDLE.
	I LOST MY NEEDLE.		THREAD NEEDLE.
	MY GOLD-EYED NEEDLE.		THREAD NEEDLE.
	IT'S MAMA'S NEEDLE.		THREAD NEEDLE.

The caller improvises MY FAVORITE NEEDLE, CAN'T FIND MY NEEDLE, WHERE'S THAT NEEDLE, ... etc. Dancers respond with THREAD NEEDLE after each call.

The leader begins by dipping under the arch formed with the immediate neighbor. Since everyone is holding hands, once the leader goes under the closest neighboring arch, that arch must twist under to follow along. Remind the dancers to keep their wrists loose. They continue weaving in and out under each consecutive arch until the end of the line is reached. To make the threading less strenuous, weave under every other arch, or every third arch. Be sure to go under the arch made by the last two people in line. The singing continues until everyone has progressed through the arches. Once at a farewell party on a large grassy playing field, ninety children and adults of all ages successfully "threaded" all around the field.

The second part continues the saga of something borrowed that has not been returned. "I am going to wind up this bunkum," means that I am going to get back that something I lent. "Bunkum" means "borrowing."

GOING TO WIND UP-A THIS BUNKUM, BUNKUM,
WIND UP-A THIS BUNKUM.
WIND UP-A THIS BUNKUM, BUNKUM, WIND UP-A THIS BUNKUM.

The leader stands still while the last one in line now leads the line. Everyone holds hands all the while as they sing and spiral around and around the stationary leader until they have formed a tight spiral knot.

GOING TO SHAKE DOWN-A THIS BUNKUM, BUNKUM,
SHAKE DOWN-A THIS BUNKUM,
SHAKE DOWN-A THIS BUNKUM, BUNKUM, SHAKE DOWN-A THIS BUNKUM.

Everyone in the tight spiral jumps up and down together for a good shaking, as they continue to hold hands. The final verse begins:

GOING TO UNWIND-A THIS BUNKUM, BUNKUM, UNWIND-A THIS BUNKUM.
UNWIND-A THIS BUNKUM, BUNKUM, UNWIND-A THIS BUNKUM.

The spiral unwinds led by the last one in line until the song finishes. Even though this game has many similarities to the Thread the Needle game, Bessie Jones insists it is unique. The order of the game, described in *Step It Down*, is: Before the first verse is sung, the leader says, "Neighbor, neighbor, lend me your hatchet." The last one in line replies: "Neighbor, neighbor, step and get it." After the first verse is sung, the last one in line says: "Neighbor, neighbor, send me my hatchet." The leader replies, "Neighbor, neighbor, I ain't got it." The dancers then wind up, shake up, and unwind as the song proceeds.

Line game
Age 7 and older

The Washerwomen

F · · · · · · · C

We watch one lit - tle foot, and we watch one lit - tle shoe, and

C G7 C G7 C F

see what the bus - y wash - er- wom - en do. They are wash - ing, they're wash - ing, they're

F C G7 C G7 C

wash - ing all day through. They're wash - ing, they're wash - ing, they're wash - ing all day through.

English

The wise old art of housekeeping is filled with rituals that nurture and strengthen children. Although many household chores have been transformed by mechanical aids, the powerful simplicity of their archetypal gestures nurture young children. This singing game invites children into the satisfying rhythmic work of busy washerwomen throughout the world. Authentic gestures are essential for children to experience the full pleasure of this singing game. To begin, the children stand and sing.

WE WATCH ONE LITTLE FOOT,
AND WE WATCH ONE LITTLE SHOE,
AND SEE WHAT THE BUSY WASHERWOMEN DO.

All the children extend their right foot forward and back, alternately with their left foot.

THEY ARE WASHING, THEY'RE WASHING,
THEY'RE WASHING ALL DAY THROUGH.
THEY'RE WASHING, THEY'RE WASHING,
THEY'RE WASHING ALL DAY THROUGH.

The children mime washing clothes on a washboard.

WE WATCH ONE LITTLE FOOT,
AND WE WATCH ONE LITTLE SHOE,
AND SEE WHAT THE BUSY WASHERWOMEN DO.

The children move their feet forward and back, as in first verse. Everyone continues singing each verse with appropriately mimed gestures.

THEY ARE WRINGING...
DRYING...
MENDING...
IRONING...
RESTING...
DANCING...
ALL DAY THROUGH.

For the youngest children, simply join hands in a circle, moving to the left, and stopping to mime the actions. SHOW ME YOUR FOOT, AND SHOW ME YOUR SHOE can be used as alternate words for the first line.

The format of this song can enhance birthday celebrations for children six and older. The birthday child stands in the middle and performs actions for the rest of the circle to imitate. For instance, AND SEE WHAT THE BIRTHDAY CHILD CAN DO... SHE'S CLAPPING... SHE'S SKIPPING... The birthday child may choose a friend to join her in the center. The circle sings: SEE WHAT THE BIRTHDAY CHILD'S FRIEND(S) CAN DO (or ...THE BIRTHDAY CHILD'S MOTHER CAN DO, or ...THE BIRTHDAY CHILD'S TEACHER CAN DO).

Circle game
Adaptable for age 4 and older

We Are the Romans

Have you an-y bread and wine? For we are the Ro - mans;

Have you an-y bread and wine? For we are the Ro - man sol - diers.

English

Dances with two lines facing each other can turn into duels, as one line steps forward to challenge the other. In this dance history replays. It is possible an ancient border conflict between the Roman soldiers and the English royal army is the original inspiration for this feisty musical confrontation. This song is sung as a dialogue. To begin, two lines of equal number face each other, one side the English and the other side the Romans.

HAVE YOU ANY BREAD AND WINE?
FOR WE ARE THE ROMANS;
HAVE YOU ANY BREAD AND WINE?
FOR WE ARE THE ROMAN SOLDIERS.

The Romans take eight steps to advance toward the English who stand still and alert, and eight steps to retreat.

YES, WE HAVE SOME BREAD AND WINE,
FOR WE ARE THE ENGLISH;
YES, WE HAVE SOME BREAD AND WINE,
FOR WE ARE THE ENGLISH SOLDIERS.

The English advance and retreat eight steps each. English and Romans continue to advance and retreat when it is their turn to sing.

THEN WE WILL HAVE ONE CUP FULL, FOR WE ARE THE ROMANS...

NO, YOU WON'T HAVE ONE CUP FULL, FOR WE ARE THE ENGLISH...

THEN WE WILL HAVE TWO CUPS FULL, FOR WE ARE THE ROMANS...

NO, YOU WON'T HAVE TWO CUPS FULL, FOR WE ARE THE ENGLISH...

WE WILL TELL THE POPE OF YOU, FOR WE ARE THE ROMANS...

WE DON'T CARE FOR THE POPE OR YOU, FOR WE ARE THE ENGLISH...

WE WILL TELL THE KING OF YOU, FOR WE ARE THE ROMANS...

WE DON'T CARE FOR THE KING OR YOU, FOR WE ARE THE ENGLISH...

WE WILL SEND OUR CATS TO SCRATCH, FOR WE ARE THE ROMANS...

WE DON'T CARE FOR YOUR CATS OR YOU, FOR WE ARE THE ENGLISH...

WE WILL SEND OUR DOGS TO BITE, FOR WE ARE THE ROMANS...

WE DON'T CARE FOR YOUR DOGS OR YOU, FOR WE ARE THE ENGLISH...

ARE YOU READY FOR A FIGHT? FOR WE ARE THE ROMANS...

YES, WE'RE READY FOR A FIGHT, FOR WE ARE THE ENGLISH...
All say, "SHOOT, BANG, FIRE!"
Each player tries to pull his opposite opponent over to his own side.

NOW WE'VE ONLY GOT ONE ARM,
FOR WE ARE THE ENGLISH/ROMANS...
All players form one circle, sing together and mime the appropriate wounds.

NOW WE'VE ONLY GOT ONE LEG, FOR WE ARE THE ENGLISH/ROMANS...

NOW WE'VE ONLY GOT ONE EYE, FOR WE ARE THE ENGLISH/ROMANS...

NOW WE ALL MUST DROP DOWN DEAD,
FOR WE ARE THE ENGLISH/ROMANS...

NOW WE'RE ALL MADE WELL AGAIN,
FOR WE ARE THE ENGLISH/ROMANS.
NOW WE'RE ALL MADE WELL AGAIN,
FOR WE ARE THE ENGLISH/ROMAN SOLDIERS.

Everyone jumps up and circles round together. This is a lively confrontation! One can organize and choreograph the battle to suit the ages: pulling one's opponent across a designated line at a signal, all hopping on one leg and trying to push opponents off balance, and so on.

Line game
Age 7 and older

Occupations

When I was Two

When I was two, I buck-led my shoe the day I went to sea. I jumped a-board the pi - rate ship, and the cap - tain said to me, "We're go - ing this way, that way, for - wards and back - wards, o - ver the I - rish Sea."

English

This English game appeals to the active spirit. For many children, the mere mention of jumping aboard a pirate ship incites enthusiasm. To begin, the children stand freely scattered about the room.

WHEN I WAS TWO, I BUCKLED MY SHOE THE DAY I WENT TO SEA.
The children mime buckling a shoe.

I JUMPED ABOARD THE PIRATE SHIP,
Everyone jumps in place.

AND THE CAPTAIN SAID TO ME,
Everyone salutes.

"WE'RE GOING THIS WAY, THAT WAY,
They sway their arms to the right, then to the left.

FORWARDS AND BACKWARDS,
Arms sway forwards, then backwards,

OVER THE IRISH SEA."
Everyone turns around in place and gets ready to start again.

The children continue miming actions appropriately on the following verses and repeat the above pattern for the chorus.

WHEN I WAS THREE, I CLIMBED A TREE THE DAY I WENT TO SEA.
I JUMPED ABOARD THE PIRATE SHIP AND THE CAPTAIN SAID TO ME,
"WE'RE GOING THIS WAY, THAT WAY, FORWARDS AND BACKWARDS,
OVER THE IRISH SEA."

WHEN I WAS FOUR, I SHUT THE DOOR...
WHEN I WAS FIVE, I LOOKED IN A HIVE...
WHEN I WAS SIX, I PICKED UP SOME STICKS...
WHEN I WAS SEVEN, I WENT TO HEAVEN...
For the final verse, the children lie down on their backs, then spring up on I JUMPED ABOARD.

This song can continue for as long as your enthusiasm and rhymes last.

Individual dance
Age 5 and older

Occupations

As children return to school in the fall, singing games quickly rekindle a sense of community. The harvest is gathered and the leaves are changing colors and falling. As the earth prepares to rest, the children's courage to learn quickens. Singing games often help facilitate academic goals. Their language is rich in pictures and rhymes. They provide opportunities for the children to experience in a natural way the necessary steps in phonemic awareness, comprehension, and articulation. As they count and step, the rhythmic beat of the music lays a foundation for the enjoyment of mathematics. Singing games in which the forms call for players to be "added," "subtracted," "multiplied" or "divided" are multi-sensory learning aids, as in *Five Little Leaves*. Those about the seasons portray science concepts in action, as in *Wind Up the Apple Tree*, and others from different regions enliven social studies lessons. When diverse cultures are danced and sung, the children also learn tolerance for their personal differences. As the autumn weather becomes increasingly unpredictable and hazardous, steady practice of singing games instills good manners and self-esteem in all.

The Turnip

INTRODUCTION

VERSE 1. Grand - fa - ther plants a tur - nip seed, hi di - dle die. He
VERSE 6. Tra la la la la la la la la Tra la la la la Tra

plants it in the earth so deep, hi - did - dle - die. Grow, my tur - nip, big and sweet,
la la la al la la la la tra la la la.

grow, my tur - nip, grow. Grand - fa - ther goes to pull it out, hi - did - dle - die. But

VERSES 1, 2, 3 & 4

tur - nip is so big and stout, hi - did - dle - die.
1. Grand - mo - ther, quick - ly come to me,
2. The grand - mother calls to the grand - child:
3. The grand - child calls to the dog:
4. The dog calls to the cat:

You help me pull. Ha - rook, ha - rook, ha - rook - dee - rook, the tur - nip will not move. The

VERSE 5

cat calls to the mouse, You help me pull. The mouse comes run - ning, one, two, three, and

pul - ling hard as hard can be, ha - rook, ha - rook, ha - rook. Plop! Now the tur - nip's out.

Melody and lyrics by Suse König, translated by B. Goldman
Used by permission

A saying from the Jewish Talmud is: Let the lesson you study be like a song. Stories in song enliven the original tale and deepen the experience. The familiar motif of this folk-tale is found in many countries. Small children take courage and revel in the thought that a tiny mouse could outdo a whole line of those who are bigger and stronger. First practice this song for several days with simple gestures as the children are seated in a circle. To play the singing game, the children sit or stand in a circle. To help the story move along, the teacher chooses the characters as they appear. Everyone sings:

Introduction:
GRANDFATHER PLANTS A TURNIP SEED, HI DIDDLE DIE.
HE PLANTS IT IN THE EARTH SO DEEP, HI DIDDLE DIE.
One child is chosen to be the little turnip seed and curls up on the floor. Another child as the grandfather mimes planting the seed and patting down the earth around the seed. The circle of children mimes the actions.

GROW, MY TURNIP, BIG AND SWEET, GROW, MY TURNIP, GROW.
The turnip sits up straight. Grandfather gestures with his arms how big the turnip is growing.

GRANDFATHER GOES TO PULL IT OUT, HI DIDDLE DIE.
BUT TURNIP IS SO BIG AND STOUT, HI DIDDLE DIE.
Grandfather places his hands on the turnip's shoulders and pulls. Grandfather gestures how big the turnip is!

Verse one:
GRANDMOTHER, QUICKLY COME TO ME, YOU HELP ME PULL.
Grandfather gestures to Grandmother.

HA-ROOK, HA-ROOK, HA-ROOK-DEE-ROOK,
THE TURNIP WILL NOT MOVE.
Grandmother places her hands on Grandfather's shoulders and tries to pull. They rock gently back and forth. The grandparents gesture that they are not strong enough to pull out the turnip and need help.

Verse two:
THE GRANDMOTHER CALLS TO THE GRANDCHILD:
YOU HELP ME PULL.
HA-ROOK, HA-ROOK, HA-ROOK-DEE-ROOK,
THE TURNIP WILL NOT MOVE.
The grandchild places hands on Grandmother's shoulders while her hands remain on Grandfather's shoulders. Together they try to pull out the firmly seated turnip and cannot.

Verse three:
THE GRANDCHILD CALLS TO THE DOG...

Verse four:
THE DOG CALLS TO THE CAT...

Verse five:

THE CAT CALLS TO THE MOUSE: YOU HELP ME PULL!
THE MOUSE COMES RUNNING, ONE, TWO, THREE,
AND PULLING HARD AS HARD CAN BE,
HA-ROOK, HA-ROOK, HA-ROOK, PLOP!
NOW THE TURNIP'S OUT!

The mouse joins the line, gives a successful tug, and everyone falls over.

Verse six:

TRA LA LA LA LA LA LA LA TRA LA LA LA.
TRA LA LA LA LA LA LA LA TRA LA LA LA.

Immediately the children get up and with the others in the larger circle, join hands to circle left. This last circling is very important to regain a sense of order.

Several turnips, each tended by a grandfather, can start the game when the group is large. A sandy beach or grassy lawn transform this classroom game into an outdoor game. A Halloween variation of this game with older children is to have an old witch plant a haunted pumpkin. She can't pull it off the vine, so she asks her spooky friends to help her.

A singing play
Age 5 and older

Wind Up the Apple Tree

Wind up the ap - ple tree. Wind up the ap - ple tree.

Ap - ples green and ap - ples red.

Adapted from the American

Winding spirals are a powerful force in nature, an archetype children love to experience. After singing this song for many years, to my dismay at first, I discovered I had been singing and teaching it incorrectly. However, this version has stuck, and I offer it to you in respect for the evolving oral tradition. To begin, the dancers join hands in a circle. Everyone sings as the leader slowly begins to spiral inward.

WIND UP THE APPLE TREE.
WIND UP THE APPLE TREE.
APPLES GREEN AND APPLES RED.

The leader drops the hand of the child on the left, keeping hold of the hand of the child on the right. Moving at a comfortable pace to the left, the leader pulls everyone in a spiral, staying close to the inside of the circle and gradually winding inward until no one can move. The old versions say that when the children are completely clumped together, they jump up and down and fall over. We enjoy unwinding the spiral. The leader may unwind the spiral, just as it was made, or make a shortcut through arches made by two or three children. The secret is to make sure that the final arch is made by the last two children in the spiral, ensuring that everyone goes through at least one arch.

This game is a wonderful companion to *Old Roger* because they both evoke apple orchards. Children enjoy inventing their own verses, so they can play this game in all seasons.

WIND UP THE HAUNTED TREE,
APPLES WORMY AND APPLES ROTTEN...

WIND UP THE SPRINGTIME TREE,
BLOSSOMS WHITE AND BLOSSOMS PINK...

Spiral dance
Age 5 and older

Fall   55

Five Little Leaves

Five lit-tle leaves so hap-py and gay, Were

danc — ing a — bout on a tree one day.

SPOKEN

Old bro-ther wind came whoo-shing through the town, One lit-tle leaf came tum-bl-ing down.

American

Sometimes a singing game can be played first as a finger game. In the autumn in the kindergarten, I introduce this game when the children are seated in a circle. Holding up one hand, the children mime "the dancing leaves," as the other hand becomes "old brother wind," swirling and tapping five finger-leaves in turn, to send each one dancing downward. After many days of repeating the song in this way with gestures, the children are ready for the dance.

**FIVE LITTLE LEAVES SO HAPPY AND GAY,
WERE DANCING ABOUT ON A TREE ONE DAY.**
All the children stand in a circle and sing. Five children are chosen to dance in the middle.

OLD BROTHER WIND CAME WHOOSHING THROUGH THE TOWN,
A child is chosen to be the wind. This line is spoken as the wind dances around the five leaves with a scarf.

ONE LITTLE LEAF CAME TUMBLING DOWN.
The singing resumes as the wind gently places the scarf on one of the leaf-children. The little "leaf" quietly falls to the ground.

**FOUR LITTLE LEAVES...
THREE LITTLE LEAVES...
TWO LITTLE LEAVES...
ONE LITTLE LEAF...**

A variation for older children calls for one child to be chosen as the tree. This child holds five long ribbons in hand. These ribbons become branches as a leaf-child holds onto the other end. Another variation for children seven years and older brings the children into a standing circle. Five children are chosen and stand with their backs to the center to form the trunk of a great tree. Each part of the trunk holds a ribbon for a branch. At the end of each branch is a dancing leaf. Continue the game as before, with the whooshing wind and the falling leaves. The advantage of this version is that it provides opportunities for at least eleven children to have a special role, five for the trunk and branches, five for the leaves, and one or more for the wind.

Circle dance
Age 5 and older

Intery Mintery Cuttery Corn

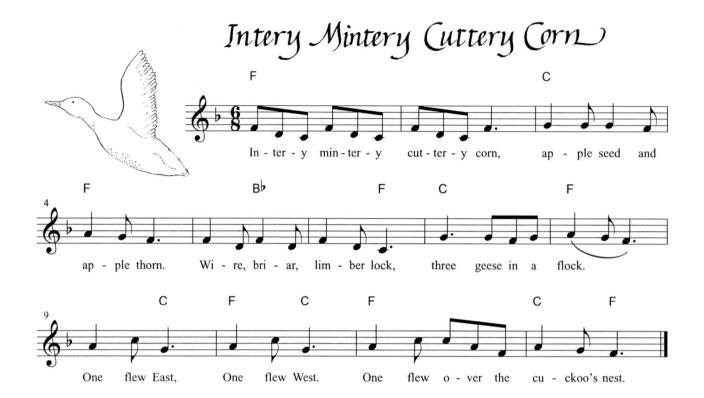

In - ter - y min - ter - y cut - ter - y corn, ap - ple seed and ap - ple thorn. Wi - re, bri - ar, lim - ber lock, three geese in a flock. One flew East, One flew West. One flew o - ver the cu - ckoo's nest.

Mother Goose rhyme, melody by George Emlen
Used by permission

Rhymes for the youngest children attune them to the delights of delicious speech. The words of this traditional nursery rhyme give their lips and tongues a calisthenic fling. George Emlen, a master musician and experienced director of many exemplary community celebrations, composed this catchy tune for the local school children in Blue Hill, Maine. His song inspired me to create this dance. To begin, the children stand in groups of three.

INTERY MINTERY CUTTERY CORN,

The dancers extend their right heel out in front of them on INTERY, and return it to place on MINTERY.
Repeat the same pattern for CUTTERY and CORN.

APPLE SEED AND APPLE THORN.

All slap their thighs (called "patch"), clap their hands, patch and clap.

WIRE, BRIAR, LIMBER LOCK,
THREE GEESE IN A FLOCK.

The three children join hands and circle to the left.

ONE FLEW EAST,

With all hands joined, two children, A and B, raise hands to form an arch under which the third one, C, ducks quickly under and steps backward to place without letting go of hands.

ONE FLEW WEST,

All keep hands joined while B and C form an arch and A ducks under it and returns to place as described above.

ONE FLEW OVER THE CUCKOO'S NEST.

All keep hands joined while C and A form arch, and B ducks under it and returns to place as described above.

A variation for older children is for the last child B on ONE FLEW OVER THE CUCKOO'S NEST to drop hands, fly under the arch formed by C and A, and join another three-some, instead of returning back to place. In this version, the game begins again with all the Bs in a new nest. Make sure that each child gets a chance to fly. One way is to say, "If you have newly arrived in this nest, you are the first cuckoo to fly under."

Circle game
Age 6 and older

Old Roger

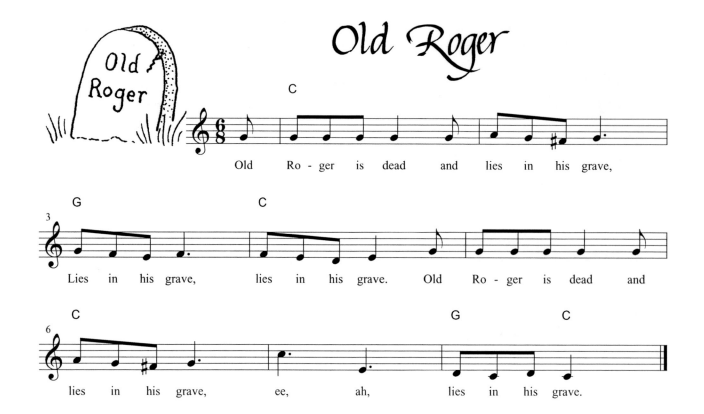

Old Ro - ger is dead and lies in his grave,

Lies in his grave, lies in his grave. Old Ro - ger is dead and

lies in his grave, ee, ah, lies in his grave.

English

Singing Games

Singing games often have roots in folk traditions and stir intuitive understanding. This singing game affirms our inherent sense of the living spirit in the natural world. Even today many families and communities plant a tree as a memorial, and thus create a sacred space. To begin, the children stand in a circle holding hands and sing:

OLD ROGER IS DEAD AND LIES IN HIS GRAVE,
LIES IN HIS GRAVE, LIES IN HIS GRAVE.
OLD ROGER IS DEAD AND LIES IN HIS GRAVE,
EE, AH, LIES IN HIS GRAVE.

The children circle to the left, as the child who has been chosen to be old Roger lies in the middle of the circle.

THEY PLANTED AN APPLE TREE OVER HIS HEAD...

The children mime planting an apple tree by digging rhythmically with a shovel.

THE APPLES GREW RIPE AND READY TO FALL...

They stand tall and stretch their arms up and hold an imaginary apple in their hands.

THE APPLES GREW RIPE AND ALL TUMBLED DOWN...

The children mime their imaginary apples falling to the ground on the word DOWN.

THERE CAME AN OLD WOMAN A-PICKING THEM UP...

A child is chosen from the circle to be an Old Woman. She bends over to pick up the apples.

OLD ROGER GOT UP AND GAVE HER A WHACK...

Old Roger stands up and chases the Old Woman around the inside of the circle. He pretends to give her a whack on the word WHACK, by clapping his hands.

WHICH MADE THE OLD WOMAN GO HIPPITY-HOP...

Old Roger returns to his grave in the middle of the circle. The Old Woman and all the other children hippity-hop in place.

If playing with parents and children together, the parents can be one character and the children the other. For example, the fathers, grandfathers, and other men can play old Roger, as the mothers, grandmothers, and other women portray the Old Woman. It adds to the spirit of fun to change roles! Instead of having just one Old Roger and Old Woman, several players can play these parts each time.

Circle game
Age 5 and older

WINTER

Dancing warms and invigorates, bringing a cozy and exhilarating sense of community to surprisingly diverse groups and settings. No gathering of my family is complete without it. No matter what the weather may be outside, singing games create a healthy climate in which children and teachers thrive. On a rainy or snowy morning at school, their predictable forms and patterns help children to channel their energies into purposeful movement. Important kinesthetic skills can be practiced in a positive and friendly mood. I especially appreciate the power of the singing game when several classes have joined together. The social courtesies arise naturally through the formalities that each dance elicits. The seemingly obvious act of asking a partner to dance can be intimidating, especially for budding adolescents. The etiquette of the dance provides a stage to practice courtesies and graces. "Would you like to dance?" "Yes, thank you."

Winter festivals have inspired many cultural traditions. Which comes first, a story or a song or a dance? I like to start these celebrations with singing games, because after dancing and singing together everyone is better able to focus on the main event, whether it is a story, a reading or other presentation. In my family and classroom, we dance carols and songs of Christmas and the Jewish Festival of Lights. The beautiful communal spirit of Israeli dances and songs brings its own light to this season of darkness.

Many a carol has been danced for centuries. "Carol" is derived from a French word meaning "circle." My friends and I enjoy creating celebration dances for special occasions. Sometimes the soloist steps into the center of the circle, following an old tradition, as the rest join in with the chorus. With so many opportunities for gathering with dear friends and family during holiday seasons, take courage and start your own singing dance tradition!

Old Befana

Be - fa - na lived long a - go, long a - go, long a - go. Be -

fa - na lived long a - go, long, long a - go.

Lyrics by Margaret More, German folk melody
Used by permission

The tune of Briar Rose is so familiar that it can easily be adapted to fit other stories as well. For instance, the Italian legend of Old Befana, or the Russian Babushka, is a traditional story for January. I always tell the story for several days first. After the children know it well, I have invited Margaret More, a magical storyteller and grandmother, to come to our school. Dressed as Befana in her flowery kerchief, shawl, and apron and carrying a broom, she tells Befana's story. Then she engages the children in the following singing game, which she created. During the game, children playing the part of the Three Kings, their pages and the guiding Star can either be part of the circle or wait in a designated spot outside the circle. Simple costumes and props add to the spirit of the play.

BEFANA LIVED LONG AGO, LONG AGO, LONG AGO.
BEFANA LIVED LONG AGO, LONG, LONG AGO.

In the middle of a circle of children, Befana stands wearing a shawl or scarf, an apron and holding a broom.

ALL DAY LONG SHE SWEEP-A, SWEEP-A, SWEEPS.
SWEEP-A, SWEEP-A, SWEEPS, SWEEP-A, SWEEP-A, SWEEPS.
ALL DAY LONG SHE SWEEP-A, SWEEP-A, SWEEPS, LONG, LONG AGO.

Befana sweeps. The rest of the group can mime the actions.

ALL DAY LONG SHE BAKE-A, BAKE-A, BAKES...

Befana and group mime baking.

THERE CAME THREE KINGS A-RIDING BY...

The kings need crowns and capes long enough for attending pages to hold as they circle. A child carrying a star hanging from a long stick precedes them. The kings process around the outside of the circle or around the room, entering the circle and standing before Befana to sing the next verse.

BEFANA, WON'T YOU COME WITH US...?
THE THREE KINGS WENT RIDING BY...

Befana sweeps as the kings leave the circle and return to their starting place.

BEFANA NEVER FOUND THOSE KINGS...

Befana takes her basket of cookies and straddles her broom to search for the kings around the outside of the circle and around the room but does not find them.

NOW SHE WANDERS FAR AND WIDE...

The children in the circle lie down and sleep. Befana walks among the sleeping children, leaving little star cookies by each one. Then she puts down her basket and sweeps, as the children continue humming the song with their teachers.

Additional verses can be created, such as ONE NIGHT THERE SHONE A GREAT BIG STAR (a child who is carrying the star walks around the outside of the circle); or ALL NIGHT LONG SHE TOSSED AND TURNED (Befana mimes restless sleep).

Tomie di Paola has written and illustrated a beautiful book called *Old Befana.*

Circle play
Age 5 and older

Deck the Hall

Deck the hall with boughs of hol-ly. Fa la la la la la la la la.

'Tis the sea-son to be jol-ly. Fa la la la la la la la la.

Don we now our gay ap-par-el. Fa la la la la la la la la.

Troll the an-cient Yu le-tide car-ol. Fa la la la la la la la la.

Welsh

Singing Games

Children's healthy need to move does not rest during holidays. Their genius for movement invites us to express the different moods of old familiar songs through our limbs. I choreographed this joyous carol so parents and children could dance together. To begin, everyone chooses a partner.

DECK THE HALL WITH BOUGHS OF HOLLY.
The partners face each other, slap their thighs ("patch"), clap their hands, and then clap with their partner.

FA LA LA LA LA LA LA LA LA.
They join hands and circle once around.

'TIS THE SEASON TO BE JOLLY.
Again, the partners face each other, patch their thighs, clap their hands, and then clap with their partner.

FA LA LA LA LA LA LA LA LA.
They join hands and circle once around.

DON WE NOW OUR GAY APPAREL.
The partners extend their right foot out and back, and then their left foot out and back.

FA LA LA LA LA LA LA LA LA.
They join hands and circle once around.

TROLL THE ANCIENT YULETIDE CAROL.
Again, they extend their right foot out and back, and then their left foot out and back.

FA LA LA LA LA LA LA LA LA.
They join hands and circle once around. Continue the second verse in the same pattern.

FOLLOW ME IN MERRY MEASURE...
WHILE I TELL OF YULETIDE TREASURE...

A variation for older children is to invent more complicated clapping patterns.

Partner dance
Age 6 and older

In a Winter Garden

In a win-ter gar-den co-vered with snow, Lit-tle seeds are sleep-ing deep be-low. Here come the child-ren one, two, three, Walk-ing in the gar-den qui-et-ly. Look out! Look out! Jack Frost is a-bout. Look out! Look out! Jack Frost is a-bout. Fa-ther Sun, come and warm us with your gen-tle rays. Make it so that Jack-y Frost won't come out to play.

Melody and lyrics by Anna Rainville

Words, music, and gestures enliven for children the dynamics that play in the natural world. The contrast of sleeping seeds and the well-organized wildness of a chase ward off "cabin fever" for children confined indoors. On an icy winter morning, this game crystallized and gave us all a welcome channel for our bursting energy. To begin, the children are seated in a circle, with generous spaces between them, to form a winter garden.

**IN A WINTER GARDEN COVERED WITH SNOW,
LITTLE SEEDS ARE SLEEPING DEEP BELOW.**

Several children are chosen to be little seeds. They curl themselves up inside the circle.

**HERE COME THE CHILDREN ONE, TWO, THREE,
WALKING IN THE GARDEN QUIETLY.**

Three children are chosen to walk around the sleeping seeds.

**LOOK OUT! LOOK OUT! JACK FROST IS ABOUT.
LOOK OUT! LOOK OUT! JACK FROST IS ABOUT.**

A child is chosen to be Jack Frost. Jack Frost chases the three children in and out and around the winter garden, trying to tag and "freeze" them. When a child is tagged, he or she stands still, "frozen." Continue singing this verse over and over during the chase until all three children have been tagged.

**FATHER SUN, COME AND WARM US WITH YOUR GENTLE RAYS.
MAKE IT SO THAT JACKY FROST WON'T COME OUT TO PLAY.**

When all three children have been tagged, a child who has been chosen to be the Sun stands up and gently touches the frozen ones. Then they return to the warm circle. Simple cloths or capes can serve as costumes for the players.

A circle play
Age 4 and older

It Came Upon a Midnight Clear

Melody by Edmund H. Sears, lyrics by Richard S. Willis, 1851

Traditional holiday songs lead a secret life as dance tunes. This carol is a waltz. Its clear harmonious rhythm invites everyone into movement. As if in a sparkling light-filled ballroom, couples may swirl like galaxies as they waltz and sing this familiar tune. "It Came Upon a Midnight Clear" also lends itself to a circle dance with couples standing side by side. Many thanks to Margaret More for its choreography and the many winter evenings she has led carol dancing.

The group will harmoniously entrain as you practice the following steps until everyone is moving together. To begin, the dancers step on the left foot and swing the right foot across the left foot, then repeat the pattern starting on the right foot. Continue this alternating pattern until all the dancers are confident in this swinging motion.

Next, count 1, 2, 3, 4, 5, 6, 1, 2, 3, 4, 5, 6. The dancers bend their knees on 1 and turn around in place while counting to 6. Then the dancers step to the left and swing the right foot across, counting 1, 2, 3. Then they step to the right and swing the left counting 4, 5, 6. Everyone turns around in place for 6 counts and repeats the sequence.

Now "trees" or "angels" are designated alternately around the circle. The "trees" stand still with deep roots ready to lead the "angels" from their right to their left side, as they fly from tree to tree around the circle. Once the dancers know their parts, everyone is ready to dance the first four lines of the carol.

**IT CAME UPON A MIDNIGHT CLEAR,
THAT GLORIOUS SONG OF OLD,
FROM ANGELS BENDING NEAR THE EARTH,
TO TOUCH THEIR HARPS OF GOLD.**

Now all step left and swing the right foot across the left foot and back on the counts of 1, 2, 3. They step right and swing the left foot across the right foot and back on the counts of 4, 5, 6. Each tree guides its angel gently from its right side to the left, changing hands so the angel can turn once around as it crosses in front on the counts 1, 2, 3, 4, 5, 6. Now the trees have received a new angel on their right side, and the entire sequence continues three more times.

"PEACE ON THE EARTH, GOODWILL TO MEN,

The trees join hands and step forward to form an inner circle of archways.

FROM HEAV'N'S ALL GRACIOUS KING."

The angels step forward and stoop under the archways made by the trees so that now the angels form the inner circle.

THE WORLD IN SOLEMN STILLNESS LAY,

The trees step forward and bend under the archways made by the angels, as the trees become the inner circle again.

TO HEAR THE ANGELS SING.

The trees take one step back and place their arms over and behind the angels, to weave into one big circle.

Couples and circle dance
Age 12 and older

Jingle Bells

Traditional

Singing Games

One inclement December day, as Christmas was fast approaching, the kindergarten children I was teaching at the time spontaneously broke into a chorus of "Jingle Bells." Sensing their restless energy and raucous enthusiasm for this so familiar song, I decided to challenge them with the following choreography. To begin, the children sit on the floor in a circle with enough room on either side for a child to pass. They are the trees in a wintry forest. Choose one child to be the sleigh; lead this child by the hand in and out between the tree children as everyone sings the verse.

Verse:
> **DASHING THROUGH THE SNOW,**
> **IN A ONE-HORSE OPEN SLEIGH,**
> **O'ER THE FIELDS WE GO,**
> **LAUGHING ALL THE WAY;**
> **BELLS ON BOBTAIL RING,**
> **MAKING SPIRITS BRIGHT;**
> **WHAT FUN IT IS TO RIDE AND SING**
> **A SLEIGHING SONG TONIGHT.**

Chorus:
> **OH, JINGLE BELLS, JINGLE BELLS, JINGLE ALL THE WAY.**
> **OH, WHAT FUN IT IS TO RIDE IN A ONE-HORSE OPEN SLEIGH.**
> **JINGLE BELLS, JINGLE BELLS, JINGLE ALL THE WAY.**
> **OH, WHAT FUN IT IS TO RIDE IN A ONE-HORSE OPEN SLEIGH.**

As the chorus begins, the sleigh child skips around the outside of the circle, and returns home as the chorus ends. This is the simplest way to dance this song. Once the children are familiar with the weaving technique, the teacher no longer needs to guide the sleigh. An additional musical delight is for the sleigh child to carry jingle bells to shake while skipping. Tree children can also shake jingle bells during the chorus.

As a variation, at the end of the chorus, the sleigh chooses another child to join in on the verse as they walk in and out between the trees. They both skip around the circle during the chorus and both choose another friend to join them walking between the trees. This produces a snowballing effect, and soon everyone is following the leader, walking around the room and then skipping.

Another more complicated variation also begins with the children seated in a circle. The teacher explains, "If I say 'tree,' you sit down with your roots tucked in. If I say 'sleigh,' stand up." The teacher designates tree and sleigh alternately around the circle.   Then all the sleighs weave in and out simultaneously between the trees, and skip around the outside of the circle together.

Circle game
Age 5 and older

Oh, Hanukkah

Oh, Ha-nuk-kah, Oh Ha-nuk-kah, come light the me-no-rah.

Let's have a par-ty, we'll all dance the ho-rah. Ga-ther round the ta-ble, we'll give you a treat:

Drei-dels to play with and lat-kes to eat. And while we are play-ing the

can-dles are burn-ing low. One for each night, they will shed a sweet light to re-

mind us of days long a-go. One for each night, they will shed a sweet light to re-

mind us of days long a-go.

Yiddish folk melody

Present-day children need the experience of celebrating many faiths. The darkness of winter inspires a longing for the light. Hanukkah is the remembrance of the Hebrew people of the destruction of the temple in Jerusalem and the miraculous "eternal flame" that continued burning for eight nights with only enough oil for one night. At school one December morning as the children were soulfully singing this ancient festival song, we started spontaneously to dance. This dance arose from that happy experience. To begin, the children join hands in a circle. Everyone sings:

OH, HANUKKAH, OH HANUKKAH, COME LIGHT THE MENORAH.
LET'S HAVE A PARTY, WE'LL ALL DANCE THE HORAH.
Everyone circles to the left.

GATHER ROUND THE TABLE, WE'LL GIVE YOU A TREAT:
DREIDELS (tops) TO PLAY WITH AND LATKES (pancakes) TO EAT.
The dancers stop and face the center. All patch (slap their thighs), clap, patch, clap, patch, clap.

AND WHILE WE ARE PLAYING THE CANDLES ARE BURNING LOW.
All place their right foot forward and lean slightly toward the center, lifting their left foot off the ground behind to create a rocking sensation. They rock forwards and back four times.

ONE FOR EACH NIGHT, THEY WILL SHED A SWEET LIGHT
TO REMIND US OF DAYS LONG AGO.
ONE FOR EACH NIGHT, THEY WILL SHED A SWEET LIGHT
TO REMIND US OF DAYS LONG AGO.
All step to the right and stamp with their left foot. Then they step to the left and stamp with their right foot. This pattern is repeated six more times in rhythm to the music.

Instead of walking as you circle left, try moving with the grapevine step. The left foot always steps to the left and the right foot alternates crossing over it in front and behind. Step left, right in front. Step left, right in back. Say, "Step left, right in front. Step left, right in back." Practice very slowly and work up to a lively tempo. Challenge to make up intricate clapping patterns on GATHER ROUND.

Circle dance
Age 6 and older

The North Wind Doth Blow

The north wind doth blow and we shall have snow and
what will poor rob - in do then, poor thing? He'll sit in the barn and
keep him - self warm and hide his head un - der his wing, poor thing.

Mother Goose rhyme, English melody

Some nursery rhymes are glimpses into the secrets of nature that children often notice better than adults do. The winter scene depicted in this simple dance and song awakens tender compassion. To begin, call an inner and an outer circle of children. The inner circle represents the barn. They join hands and stand still. The outer circle represents the robin. They move left around the barn at first flapping their wings.

**THE NORTH WIND DOTH BLOW AND WE SHALL HAVE SNOW
AND WHAT WILL POOR ROBIN DO THEN, POOR THING?**

The robins fly around the barn. When the children sing POOR THING, all stop and stamp their feet twice.

**HE'LL SIT IN THE BARN AND KEEP HIMSELF WARM
AND HIDE HIS HEAD UNDER HIS WING, POOR THING.**

The barn raises its arms to form window arches and the robins fly under to the inside of the circle and hide their heads under their wings. Everyone stamps on POOR THING. Now the robins join hands and become the barn while the former barn becomes the robins. The alternating expansion and contraction of the circle offers a healthy breathing experience for the children.

For children not yet seven years old, the song may be danced in one joined circle, acting out the robin's plight. Additional simple verses about winter's creatures can extend this song, For example:

**THE NORTH WIND DOTH BLOW AND WE SHALL HAVE SNOW
AND WHAT WILL THE GRAY MOUSE DO THEN, POOR THING?
ROLLED UP IN A BALL IN HIS NEST SNUG AND SMALL
HE'LL SLEEP TIL THE WINTER IS GONE, POOR THING.**

As in the verse about the robin, younger children join hands and circle to the left. They walk together to the center of the circle, and crouch down to hide their heads for the robin, or roll up for the mouse.

**THE NORTH WIND DOTH BLOW AND WE SHALL HAVE SNOW
AND WHAT WILL THE SWALLOW DO THEN, POOR THING?
OH DO YOU NOT KNOW, SHE'S GONE LONG AGO
TO A COUNTRY MUCH WARMER THAN OURS, LUCKY THING!**

The children circle to the left and on the last line flap their wings and fly!

Circle dance
Age 4 and older

Winter   77

We are Three Wandering Travelers

We are three wan - d'ring trav' - lers out in the wind and the rain. We saw your light shin - ing so bright tapped on your win - dow pane Say - ing Let us come in, let us come in, In - to your house, we pray. Let us come in, let us come in, Please do not turn us a - way.

English

The traditional celebration of Christmas in Mexico includes a custom called Las Posadas, which means "the shelters." Processions of villagers wander through the streets carrying images of Mary and Joseph. Knocking at a door, the travelers sing and ask for shelter. At first they are refused, until at the last house they are welcomed in for a festive celebration. Although this song is English, it carries some of these themes. In December I invite my pupils and their parents to join me for a holiday party with gingerbread, tangerines and apple juice. This is one of the favorite singing games we share with our parents. To begin, three traveler children are chosen to walk around the circle of children who represent the village. Everyone sings:

WE ARE THREE WAND'RING TRAV'LERS OUT IN THE WIND AND THE RAIN.
The children stand in a circle with hands joined to become the village. The three travelers walk around the outside of the circle.

WE SAW YOUR LIGHT SHINING SO BRIGHT
The children in the circle stretch out their arms to the center and form a lamp out of their clasped hands.

TAPPED ON YOUR WINDOW PANE
SAYING LET US COME IN, LET US COME IN,
INTO YOUR HOUSE, WE PRAY.
LET US COME IN, LET US COME IN,
PLEASE DO NOT TURN US AWAY.
The travelers each stop behind a child and tap gently on their shoulders in time to the music.

NO!
The children in the circle turn around to face the travelers, stamp their feet and say NO! loudly. The game continues as the travelers again ask and are rejected. On the third time, instead of a hearty NO!, the circle children say YES! As they welcome the travelers either into the middle of the circle, or more cozily, into the little house they made by stretching their hands out, they sing:

YOU MAY COME IN, YOU MAY COME IN,
INTO OUR HOUSE WE PRAY.
YOU MAY COME IN, YOU MAY COME IN,
WE WILL NOT TURN YOU AWAY.

It is delightful when adults and children are together and reverse the roles of being travelers and villagers. For example, the parents stand still in the circle while all the children are the travelers. And then the parents become the travelers and the children the village.

Circle dance
Age 5 and older

SPRING

Our family has celebrated May Day for as long as I can remember. On the night before the celebration, three generations are busy together baking shortcake and preparing strawberries, decorating the maypole and festooning the May Queen's throne with cloths and flowers. Early on May Day morning, friends and neighbors arrive in the garden at seven o'clock to eat strawberry shortcake as we await the arrival of this year's Queen and her court. With a fanfare from our local trumpeters, she enters and greets us all. Next a playlet is performed. It features costumed harbingers of spring who confront wintry characters. At last the seasonal crown passes from winter to spring. Then the maypole dancing begins. The littlest ones begin winding up the ribbons of the maypole by walking around to the music of the fiddlers. Dancers of all ages wind and unwind the pole in a variety of weaving patterns until eight o'clock. Then the maypole is rushed into the back of a waiting van to journey up to our mountain school's festivities.

At my former school, the children gathered around the flagpole where sixth-graders as Lady Spring and King Winter re-enacted the yearly skirmish between their season realms. Afterwards, the fifth-graders, adorned with bells, danced Morris dances to wake up the earth. We followed them to the maypole, where they performed a traditional dance accompanied by fiddlers and recorder players from the various grades. All the sixth-grade girls together were May Queens, crowned with wreaths of spring flowers. As the children returned to their classrooms, they each received a long-stemmed strawberry from one of the May Queens.

On May Day in my present school, we feature dances by each grade. The first-graders dance *Here We Go Round the Maypole High* and *Come Dance Round the Maypole*. The second grade dances the *Barber's Pole*, the third grade, the *Spider's Web*. The fourth-graders perform a sword dance and the fifth grade weaves the maypole ribbons all the way down the pole, in a traditional plaited weave. The ceremony ends with English country dancing by the sixth grade, and Morris dancing by the seventh. One year the eighth grade dazzled us with an authentic English court dance from King Henry VIII's era.

SPRING

All the Birds Sing Up in the Trees

All the birds sing up in the trees Now that Spring is com - ing.

Lis - ten, lis - ten, what do they say? Spring-time is the time to be gay!

All the birds sing up in the trees Now that Spring is com - ing.

Spring is full of creative juice and joy for both children and adults. One way to channel this extraordinary force is to make up dances from beloved tunes. After singing this folk melody for several days, this dance blossomed one spring morning in the kindergarten. To begin, the children stand in a circle holding hands. Everyone sings:

**ALL THE BIRDS SING UP IN THE TREES
NOW THAT SPRING IS COMING.**
Several children are chosen to be little birds and stand in the middle of the circle. The circle moves to the left. The little birds fly around inside.

**LISTEN, LISTEN, WHAT DO THEY SAY?
SPRINGTIME IS THE TIME TO BE GAY!**
The children holding hands in the circle stop and raise their joined hands to make window arches. The little birds fly in and out through the windows.

**ALL THE BIRDS SING UP IN THE TREES
NOW THAT SPRING IS COMING.**
The little birds return to the center of the circle and the circle moves to the left.

Circle dance
Age 5 and older

Come Dance 'Round the Maypole

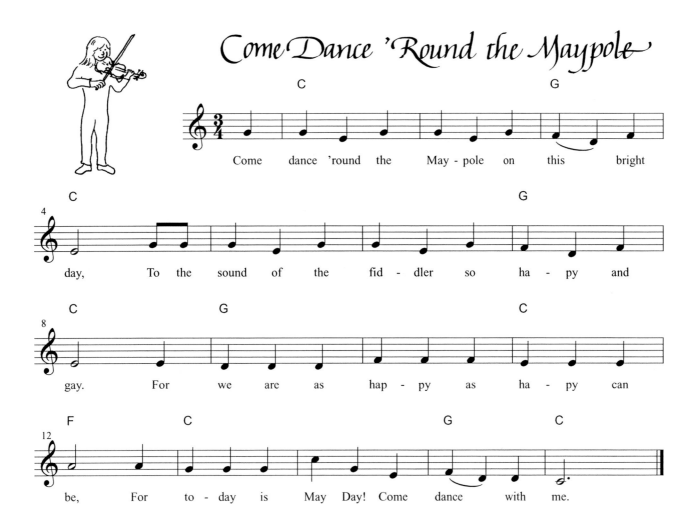

Anonymous

Familiar faces, young and old, who provide music for celebrations, expand the generous spirit of the event. Fiddles, recorders, concertinas, accordions, penny whistles, drum, and bells lift both feet and hearts and support singing voices. This song celebrates May Day musicians who accompany our dances around the maypole. Our youngest maypole dancers are invited to perform this song.

COME DANCE 'ROUND THE MAYPOLE ON THIS BRIGHT DAY,
TO THE SOUND OF THE FIDDLER SO HAPPY AND GAY.
FOR WE ARE AS HAPPY AS HAPPY CAN BE,
FOR TODAY IS MAY DAY! COME DANCE WITH ME.

The children take a ribbon from the maypole in their right hand. Holding the ribbon high above their heads, they dance by turning around in place underneath the ribbon.

Maypole dance
Age 4 and older

Spring

In and Out the Bonnie Bluebells

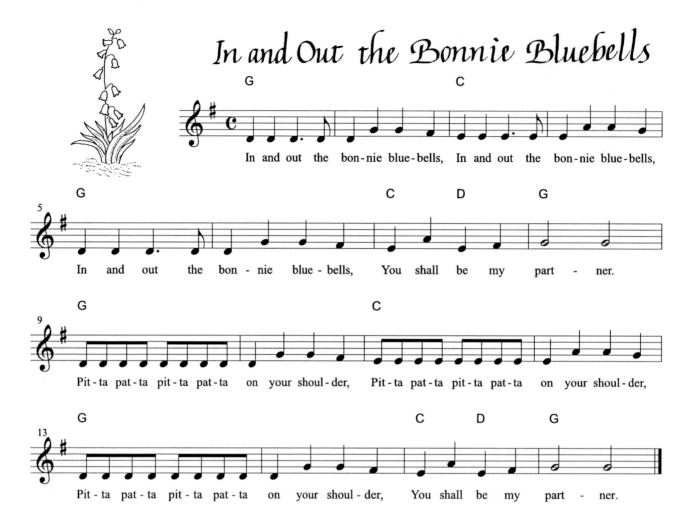

In and out the bon-nie blue-bells, In and out the bon-nie blue-bells,

In and out the bon-nie blue-bells, You shall be my part - ner.

Pit - ta pat-ta pit-ta pat-ta on your shoul-der, Pit-ta pat-ta pit-ta pat-ta on your shoul-der,

Pit - ta pat-ta pit-ta pat-ta on your shoul-der, You shall be my part - ner.

Scottish

Children especially enjoy this dance because they tap on each other's shoulders. Originally from Scotland, it is also a favorite with adults who transform the tapping into delight- ful shoulder massage. In its simplest version for the five-year-old, the children stand in a circle joining hands to start. Two children are chosen to walk around the outside of the circle as they hold hands. The singing begins:

IN AND OUT THE BONNIE BLUEBELLS,
IN AND OUT THE BONNIE BLUEBELLS,
IN AND OUT THE BONNIE BLUEBELLS,
YOU SHALL BE MY PARTNER.

The circle moves clockwise and the two children may go in the opposite direction.

PITTA PATTA PITTA PATTA ON YOUR SHOULDER,
PITTA PATTA PITTA PATTA ON YOUR SHOULDER,
PITTA PATTA PITTA PATTA ON YOUR SHOULDER,
YOU SHALL BE MY PARTNER.

Everybody stands still. The two children pitta-pat on the shoulders of a child in the circle, who then follows the two around the circle as the game continues.

Another variation for young children:
The children join hands and circle to the left. A leader is chosen to walk around outside the circle for the first eight bars. On PITTA PATTA, the circle stands still and the leader taps the shoulder once of the nearest child in front of him and then moves around the circle gently tapping the children's shoulders. The last child to be touched follows the leader around the outside as the circle moves to the left and the game begins again. Yet another variation is when the leader stands behind only one child during the PITTA PATTA.

Variation for children of six and a half years and older:
The children stand in a circle holding hands with their arms raised to form arches. One child, the leader, is chosen to weave in and out between the arches. The leader stops behind another child in the circle and, to the beat of the music, taps gently on her shoulders. As the game continues, the child who has been tapped joins hands with the leader again to weave in and out between the arches. On PITTA PATTA, they stand behind two neighboring children in the circle and tap on their shoulders. Now four children weave in and out. The meadow of bluebells (the circle) gets a little smaller. The other children rejoin hands each time as the circle contracts. Finally, there are only two children left, and they receive a gentle pitter-pattering from all the children. Alternately, two long lines can form behind each one, so that everyone receives a sweet massage at the same time. During the final verse, after everyone has been included in the line, a parent or teacher can lead the line outside to play, singing all the way.

This dance gives the children an experience of how a circle dissolves and a new circle forms. Introduce this game with a short story or a description of a meadow of blue flowers. The sense of blue can be enhanced by including blue scarves and other cloths in the dance.

Circle dance
Age 5 and older

Briar Rose

The prin-cess was a love-ly child, love-ly child, love-ly child. The prin-cess was a love-ly child, love-ly child.

German

Dancing to fairy tales invites the children to embody their rich images. I tell this story from the Grimms' collection for many days to give the children the opportunity to create their own inner pictures. Only then do we act it out in song. This is a traditional song originally from Germany, where this tale has been sung and danced for generations. To begin, choose children to be the princess, the prince, and the wicked fairy.

**THE PRINCESS WAS A LOVELY CHILD,
LOVELY CHILD, LOVELY CHILD.
THE PRINCESS WAS A LOVELY CHILD,
LOVELY CHILD.**

The children join hands and circle to the left, as the chosen characters remain part of the moving circle.

**SHE LIVED UP IN A CASTLE TALL, CASTLE TALL, CASTLE TALL.
SHE LIVED UP IN A CASTLE TALL, CASTLE TALL.**
The children stand still in a circle with their arms stretched high above their heads.

THERE CAME A WICKED FAIRY BY...
The wicked fairy steps into the circle.

OH, YOU MUST SLEEP ONE HUNDRED YEARS...
Wicked fairy wags her finger at Briar Rose, who falls asleep on the ground.

A BRIAR HEDGE GREW ALL AROUND...
The children in the circle entwine their arms to make a hedge.

THERE CAME A PRINCE A RIDING BY...
The prince skips around the outside of the circle.

THE BRIARS CHANGED TO ROSES...
The prince raises his sword arm and gently touches the briar hedge. The children untangle their arms and form arches, through which the prince enters the circle.

HE CLIMBED THE STEPS IN THE WINDING TOWER...
The prince walks around inside the circle.

HE TURNED THE LITTLE RUSTY KEY...
The prince mimes turning the key.

OH, PRINCESS WAKE AND COME WITH ME...
The prince wakes up Briar Rose by taking her hand and helping her to stand.

SO EVERYBODY'S HAPPY NOW...
The prince and Briar Rose dance together inside the circle while everyone else circles left.

Other verses can be made up out of the story. For example, the sleeping court, the futile attempts by the other princes.

Although referred to as a "wicked fairy," this character brings necessary change. She belongs to a long tradition of formidable wise women. Please refer to *Storytelling and the Art of Imagination* by Nancy Mellon.

Circle dance
Age 6 and older

Dayenu

Israeli

This is a song to celebrate the story of Passover that is described in the book of Exodus. The song celebrates Moses leading the Hebrew people out of slavery in Egypt. Dayenu means, "It would have been enough!" First the exodus succeeded, and then the Red Sea opened. Each miracle filled them with wonder and far exceeded their expectations. Although the song is at least a thousand years old, the dance sprang up freshly for a school observance.

To begin, the dancers stand in a circle holding hands.

Verse:
> **HAD HE LED US OUT OF EGYPT,**
> **ONLY LED US OUT OF EGYPT,**
> **HAD HE LED US OUT OF EGYPT,**
> **DAYENU.**

Everyone circles to the left with joined hands in a grapevine step, or just a quick walking step with young children. When I teach the grapevine step, we begin with sliding our left foot out to the side and stepping the right foot to join it. I say: "Side." Once we can progress around the circle in this step, we begin to cross the right foot in front of the left foot and then in back. I say: "Side front, side back." When everyone is moving together, we begin the first verse.

Chorus:
> **DA, DAYENU,**
> **DA, DAYENU,**
> **DA, DAYENU,**
> **DAYENU, DAYENU, DAYENU.**
>
> **DA, DAYENU,**
> **DA, DAYENU,**
> **DA, DAYENU,**
> **DAYENU, DAYENU.**

Everyone stops moving on the chorus and faces the center to patch (slap their thighs), clap their hands together, patch and clap…

Verse:
> **HAD HE MADE THE RED SEA OPEN,**
> **ONLY MADE THE RED SEA OPEN,**
> **HAD HE MADE THE RED SEA OPEN,**
> **DAYENU.**

Everyone circles left with a grapevine step on the verse and again pauses on the chorus to patch and clap.

Many variations can be improvised on the spot! For example, on the chorus, turn to a partner and patch, then clap your partner's hands, or patch, clap your own hands, clap your partner's hands, clap your own hands, and repeat this pattern.

Another possibility is to turn toward your partner in the circle and extend your right hand to do a Grand Right and Left around the circle. On the chorus, the children can be invited to make up their own challenging clapping patterns with their partners.

Especially appropriate for Passover
Circle game
Age 6 and older

Here We Go 'Round the Maypole High

F   C

Here we go 'round the May-pole high, The May-pole high, the

C   F

May-pole high. Here we go 'round the May - pole high. Let

C   F   C   F

col - ored rib - bons fly. Let col - ored rib - bons fly.

English

90   Singing Games

Young children benefit from watching older children and adults dancing together in celebration. They anticipate the time when they are ready to be steadfast, concentrated members of the dancing group. Until then, they enjoy their own age-appropriate version of the traditional maypole dance. The whole ambience of the May celebration nourishes their senses. On May Day morning the youngest children are the first to dance around the maypole with this song.

Verse one:
HERE WE GO 'ROUND THE MAYPOLE HIGH,
THE MAYPOLE HIGH, THE MAYPOLE HIGH.
HERE WE GO 'ROUND THE MAYPOLE HIGH.

The children take a ribbon from the maypole in their right hands and circle around the pole to the left, holding their ribbons high.

LET COLORED RIBBONS FLY.
LET COLORED RIBBONS FLY.

They stop and face the maypole. They sway their ribbons from side to side in the rhythm of the song.

Verse two:
SEE LADS AND LASSIES GO DANCING BY,
GO DANCING BY, GO DANCING BY.
SEE LADS AND LASSIES GO DANCING BY.

The children transfer the ribbons to their left hands, and then circle around the pole to the right until they have returned to their original places.

LET COLORED RIBBONS FLY.
LET COLORED RIBBONS FLY.

Again, they stop and face the maypole. They sway their ribbons from side to side in the rhythm of the song.

Maypole dance
Age 4 and older

Branch of Snowy May

Here's a branch of sno-wy May, A branch the fair-ies gave me.

Who would like to dance to-day, With a branch the fair-ies gave me?

Dance a-way, dance a-way, Hold-ing high the branch of May.

Dance a-way, dance a-way, Hold-ing high the branch of May.

Dutch melody, lyrics anonymous

This dance invokes the lightness of spring blossoms. "Snowy May" refers specifically to the hawthorn, which bloom prolifically along the hedgerows in England in May. For this dance, in lieu of blossoming branches of white hawthorn, I often cut long sprigs of whatever is available in the garden, or even make white tissue paper blossoms and attach them to twigs or bamboo garden stakes. I add white streamers to create more of a sense of movement. To begin the dance, two children face one another, each with a blossoming branch. They hold the two branches high to form an arch. (See the full-page illustration for Spring.) Now the singing begins:

**HERE'S A BRANCH OF SNOWY MAY,
A BRANCH THE FAIRIES GAVE ME.
WHO WOULD LIKE TO DANCE TODAY,
WITH A BRANCH THE FAIRIES GAVE ME?
DANCE AWAY, DANCE AWAY,
HOLDING HIGH THE BRANCH OF MAY.
DANCE AWAY, DANCE AWAY,
HOLDING HIGH THE BRANCH OF MAY.**

As the two children hold the flower arch, another child stands facing the arch and skips in a figure eight under the archway and around the two children.

On the last HOLDING HIGH THE BRANCH OF MAY, the skipping child stops facing the arch and bows or curtseys.

A variation for older children is to invite two skipping children to begin dancing figure eights simultaneously, but moving in opposite directions. A variation for children who are not yet seven years old, is to move clockwise in a circle with two children in the center, each holding a branch of May. On the words DANCE AWAY, the children in the outside circle stand still while the two in the center each choose a partner. The couples dance around together inside the circle until the song ends. This is one of the songs we sing at our Mother's Day celebration every year. Mothers, aunties, grandmothers hold the branches for the young dancers. Then the children hold the branches for their dancing elders. I know of early childhood teachers who adapt this song for other seasons.

Circle and partner dance
Age 5 and older

Knots of May

Here we come ga-ther-ing knots of May, knots of May, knots of May. Here we come ga-ther-ing knots of May, So ear-ly in the morn - ing.

English

"Knots of May" are the blossoms of the May tree, a variety of English white hawthorn tree. This competitive song is often referred to as "Nuts in May", which is quite inappropriate, since there are not any nuts to gather in May. "Knot" is an old English word for branch. As the song begins, two lines of dancers face each other, line A and line B. Everyone sings:

HERE WE COME GATHERING KNOTS OF MAY,
KNOTS OF MAY, KNOTS OF MAY.
HERE WE COME GATHERING KNOTS OF MAY,
SO EARLY IN THE MORNING.

Lines A and B face each other and sing while they both walk forward four steps and back four steps for each line of the verse.

WHO WILL YOU HAVE FOR KNOTS OF MAY,
KNOTS OF MAY, KNOTS OF MAY?
WHO WILL YOU HAVE FOR KNOTS OF MAY,
SO EARLY IN THE MORNING?

Line A walks forward four steps and back four steps while singing each line of the verse. Line B stands still.

WE'LL HAVE (a child's name in line A) FOR KNOTS OF MAY...

Line B walks forward four steps and back four steps as above, while line A stands still.

WHO WILL YOU HAVE TO PULL HER ACROSS?

Line A repeats the pattern above as again line B stands still.

WE'LL HAVE (a child's name in line B) TO PULL HER ACROSS...

Line B walks forward singing while line A stands still.

The two designated children meet in the middle where a line has been drawn. They place right feet toe-to-toe on the line and then take both hands. At the signal, they try to pull the other across the line. Whoever is pulled over joins the other's line and the game continues, until all the children are on one side.

An alternative ending is:

A sings **WHO WILL YOU HAVE FOR KNOTS IN MAY?**
B sings **WE'LL HAVE YOU ALL...**
A sings **WHO WILL YOU HAVE TO PULL US ACROSS?**
B sings **WE'LL HAVE US ALL TO PULL YOU ACROSS.**

Children form lines A and B, pair up across from one another, and at the signal everyone pulls! There is usually a happy jumble of children on the floor or the lawn at the end!

Line dance
Age 7 and older

Kling, Klang Gloria

Kling, klang Glo - ri - a, Ros - sel, ros - sel fi - li - a, who's

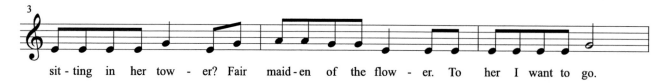

sit - ting in her tow - er? Fair maid - en of the flow - er. To her I want to go.

No, no, no. She can - not see the light of day, un - til you break the stones a - way.

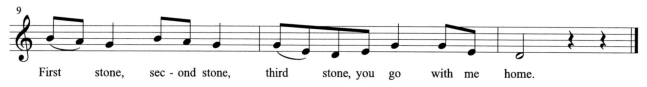

First stone, sec - ond stone, third stone, you go with me home.

Lyrics by Margret Meyerkort, German melody

Children savor the pictures evoked by wise old tales, even if their meaning has not yet dawned upon them. Moving to the rhythm of beautiful language invites them to discover important archetypes that will help them accept the challenges of growing older and wiser. The words of this song portray dynamic themes that appear in many of the greatest fairy tales. To begin, the children stand in a circle, holding hands to form a tower. Everyone sings:

KLING, KLANG GLORIA,
ROSSEL, ROSSEL FILIA,
WHO'S SITTING IN THE TOWER?
FAIR MAIDEN OF THE FLOWER.
TO HER I WANT TO GO.

A child is chosen to be the princess, who sits in the middle of the circle tower. A prince is chosen to walk counterclockwise around the outside of the tower.

NO, NO, NO.
SHE CANNOT SEE THE LIGHT OF DAY,
UNTIL YOU BREAK THE STONES AWAY.

The circle steps in closer to protect the princess.

FIRST STONE,

The prince taps one circle child on the shoulder,

SECOND STONE,

then a second child...

THIRD STONE,
YOU GO WITH ME HOME.

and a third child, who joins hands with the prince. They walk around the tower together and the song begins again. They continue until all the stones are removed. Then they sing:

KLING KLANG GLORIA,
ROSSEL, ROSSEL, FILIA,
WHO'S SITTING IN THE TOWER?
FAIR MAIDEN OF THE FLOWER.
TO HER I WANT TO GO.
YES, YES, YES!
LA, LA, LA, LA, LA...

The princess and prince dance around together in the middle of the circle while the children clap their hands. If there are many children, have the first, second, and third stones all join the prince at the same time. The tower can remain stationary or circle left, while the prince circles right. This game is a lovely ending to a story you make up about a princess captive in a stone tower.

Circle dance
Age 6 and older

Maypole Dances

Britches Full of Stitches

(One of many tunes that can be used for a maypole dance)

Irish polka

MAYPOLE DANCE FOR OLDER CHILDREN AND ADULTS

Every May Day morning calls for a joyous dance. You will need a tall maypole with an even number of long ribbons. I recommend using only two colors so that the dancers and audience of revelers can easily follow the intricate weaving patterns. I chose leafy green and daffodil yellow for our maypole one year and have maintained this spring color scheme ever since. Here are six different possibilities for your May celebrations. Invite local musicians or older students to accompany the dancing. Start with having everyone practice the Grand Right and Left, first by taking one another's hands in passing and then without touching one another. This effectively helps the dancers prepare for the challenge of weaving in and out while holding onto ribbons. Once this has been mastered by the whole group, with confidence each dancer takes hold of a ribbon in the right hand and bows to the maypole, the May Queen and the musicians, and the dance begins.

INS AND OUTS

Everyone walks or skips four steps toward the pole and four steps back to place. This pattern repeats.

Then the dancers holding the green ribbons (Greens) walk or skip four steps in and out again while the dancers holding the yellow ribbons (Yellows) stand in place. Now the Yellows step four steps in and four steps out while the Greens stand in place. This sequence repeats once.

The Greens step in four while the Yellows stay in place. While the Yellows begin stepping in, the Greens step back. Repeat this sequence until each group has stepped in and out four times.

BARBER'S POLE

The Greens take three steps in and turn right. The Yellows remain in place and turn left. Then holding their yellow ribbons they skip once around pole while Greens stand still. When the Yellows are back to their places, they stand still and the Greens skip once around the pole. This pattern continues until the pole is wound up into a colorful wrapping. Then the dancers reverse all of the above to unwind the ribbons for the next dance. Alternative: Greens and Yellows make circles simultaneuosly.

SPIDER'S WEB

The Greens stand still and the Yellows weave around them to create a web. To do this, the Greens take two steps forward. The Yellows stand behind the Green to their left. The Yellows hold their ribbons tautly and going under the green ribbon, dance around the Greens in a loop encircling each Green starting to the left. After returning to place, the Yellows continue to the next Green on the left to repeat pattern. After the web is woven the Yellows turn and undo the weaving by reversing the sequence.

WEAVING FINALE

The Greens turn to the left and the Yellows turn to the right facing the Greens. Each color continues moving in opposite directions around the Maypole. The Greens hold their ribbons high while the Yellows dance underneath the green ribbons. Then the Yellows hold their ribbons high while the Greens dance under the yellow ribbons. They repeat this pattern weaving over and under, until the ribbons enclose the pole in a crisscross weave.

FAREWELL

The dancers face the pole still holding on to the last few inches of their ribbons. They take four steps into the middle and drop the ribbons. Then they join hands and circle around the pole. One designated dancer lets go of the hand of the neighbor to the right and leads the dancers off.

It is important to keep the ribbons untwisted and taut. As the dancers keep their eyes focused on their ribbons, it is easier to remember the pattern of over, then under, then over, then under. The dancers must each keep a steady pace.

Stop the dancers when the weaving pattern is disrupted. They must reverse directions until the pattern is clear. This is easier if they look up at the pole to catch any problems during the unweaving before they resume.

Sometimes a crowd of 100 people attends our May celebrations. In order to give everyone a chance to dance, each group of dancers winds the pole to a certain point. Then the caller signals for the dancers to reverse directions and unwind the pole so the ribbons are free for the next group. The last group of dancers can wind the ribbons all the way down the pole.

Water, Water Wallflower

Wat-er, wat-er wall-flow'r, grow-ing up so high,

We are all God's chil-dren and we all must die. Ex-cept-ing for (child's name) the

fair-est of us all: She/He can dance and she/he can sing and she/he can wear a

wed-ding ring. Fie, fie, fie for shame, Turn your face to the wall a-gain.

Scottish

This is another song that raises eyebrows among adults but is thoroughly loved by the children. As children play without interference, they naturally play out the cycle of life. Wallflowers received their name from the sheltering stone walls where they thrive. Their delicate colors and aroma remind us of the fragility of earthly life and our human need to learn to stand firmly in our own integrity. During this singing game, children practice facing away from the group toward the unknown. For the same reasons, adults enjoy this game at parties, meetings, and even at very large community gatherings. To begin, everyone joins hands in a circle and moves to the left, singing:

**WATER, WATER WALLFLOWER, GROWING UP SO HIGH,
WE ARE ALL GOD'S CHILDREN AND WE ALL MUST DIE.
EXCEPTING FOR (Child's name) THE FAIREST OF US ALL:
SHE CAN DANCE AND SHE CAN SING AND SHE CAN WEAR A WEDDING RING.**

The teacher sings the name of one child during the third line. This child dances around the inside of the circle. The circle children clap their hands and tap their toes.

FIE, FIE, FIE FOR SHAME, TURN YOUR FACE TO THE WALL AGAIN.

The dancing child returns to place and takes hands with the circle facing outward away from the other children. The song continues until everyone is facing outward. If the group is exceptionally large, the names of two or three children can be called at the same time to dance inside the circle. When everyone has turned outward away from the center, still holding hands, sing the following verse:

**WATER, WATER WALLFLOWER, GROWING UP SO HIGH,
WE ARE ALL GOD'S CHILDREN, AND WE ALL MUST DIE.
EXCEPTING FOR ALL OF US, THE FAIREST OF US ALL:
WE CAN DANCE AND WE CAN SING
AND WE CAN WEAR A WEDDING RING.
FIE, FIE, FIE FOR SHAME, WE'RE ALL TURNED BACK ROUND AGAIN.**

All the children are standing in a circle with their backs to the center, holding hands. The teacher leads the circle through an archway made by two children, who raise their joined hands together. As she walks backward, she pulls all the children gently through the archway until they are all turned back round again and standing in the original circle, ready to start the game once more.

Circle dance
Age 6 and older

The Cuckoo and the Donkey

The cu-ckoo and the don-key, They quar-relled one fine day, As to who could bet-ter sing, As to who could bet-ter sing, In the love-ly month of May, In the love-ly month of May.

German

Dancing in two lines that face one another is like a conversation. Although the rascally cuckoo is fast becoming an endangered species, this dynamic song preserves its place in our folk heritage. To begin, the children stand in two lines facing each other and sing:

Verse one:
> **THE CUCKOO AND THE DONKEY,**
> **THEY QUARRELLED ONE FINE DAY,**

One line is designated as the cuckoos and the other as the donkeys. During this verse, the cuckoos take eight steps forward.

> **AS TO WHO COULD BETTER SING,**
> **AS TO WHO COULD BETTER SING,**

The donkeys take eight steps forward to meet the cuckoos in the middle.

> **IN THE LOVELY MONTH OF MAY,**
> **IN THE LOVELY MONTH OF MAY.**

The cuckoos and the donkeys take eight steps backward to their original positions.

Verse two:
> **THE CUCKOO SAID, "HEAR ME SING,"**
> **AND SOON BEGAN TO CALL,**

The cuckoos take eight steps forward.

> **"BUT I CAN DO IT BETTER,"**
> **"BUT I CAN DO IT BETTER,"**

The donkeys take eight steps forward.

> **SAID THE DONKEY, WITH "HEE-HAW,"**
> **SAID THE DONKEY, WITH "HEE-HAW."**

The cuckoos and the donkeys take eight steps back to their original positions.

Verse three:
> **THESE SOUNDS SO SWEET AND LOVELY,**
> **ONE HEARD THEM FAR AND WIDE,**

The cuckoos take eight steps forward.

> **THEY SANG SO WELL TOGETHER,**
> **THEY SANG SO WELL TOGETHER,**

The donkeys take eight steps forward.

> **"CUCKOO, CUCKOO."**

The cuckoos keep advancing, while pushing the donkeys back.

> **"HEE-HAW."**

The donkeys keep advancing, while pushing the cuckoos back.

> **"CUCKOO, CUCKOO."**

The cuckoos keep advancing, while pushing the donkeys back.

> **"HEE-HAW!"**

The donkeys keep advancing, while pushing the cuckoos back.

Line dance
Age 7 and older

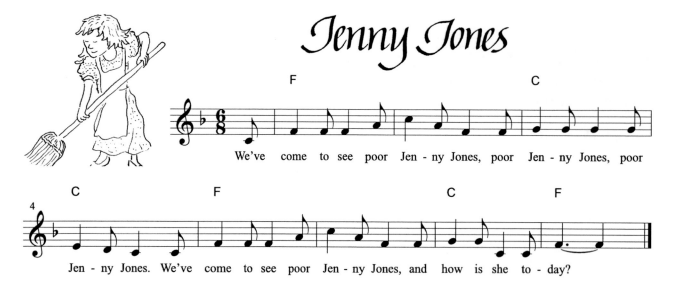

Jenny Jones

We've come to see poor Jen-ny Jones, poor Jen-ny Jones, poor Jen-ny Jones. We've come to see poor Jen-ny Jones, and how is she to-day?

English

As well as playing with life, children need to play with death. The popularity of this singing game from England over many generations attests to the courage for truth in children. Early spring with abundance of new life sprouting out of winter's darkness and sleep, is an especially appropriate time to play this game. Jenny Jones can become Jimmy Jones, and her caretakers can be either mother or father. Peter and Iona Opie, in their classic The Singing Game, *note that the rhythmic "to-ing and fro-ing" of the spoken and sung dialogue together with "the mock solemnity of a funeral" create a universal appeal. To begin, the children stand together in a circle and join hands. Everyone sings:*

WE'VE COME TO SEE POOR JENNY JONES,
Two children are chosen to be the parent and child and stand in the center of the circle. The children in the circle take four steps forward.

POOR JENNY JONES, POOR JENNY JONES.
WE'VE COME TO SEE POOR JENNY JONES,
AND HOW IS SHE TODAY?
The circle takes four steps backwards to place, then another four into the center and four back.

CAN WE SEE JENNY JONES TODAY?
The circle stands still and speaks this question.

OH NO, YOU CAN'T SEE JENNY JONES TODAY. SHE'S BUSY WASHING.
The parent replies.

JENNY JONES IS WASHING, WASHING, WASHING.
JENNY JONES IS WASHING. WE CAN'T SEE HER TODAY.
All the children mime washing, while singing.

**WE'VE COME TO SEE POOR JENNY JONES,
POOR JENNY JONES, POOR JENNY JONES.
WE'VE COME TO SEE POOR JENNY JONES,
AND HOW IS SHE TODAY?**
The circle walks four steps in and out, in and out to place.

CAN WE SEE JENNY JONES TODAY?
Again the circle asks this question.

OH NO, YOU CAN'T SEE JENNY JONES. SHE'S BUSY IRONING (or some other activity).
The parent replies.

JENNY JONES IS IRONING, IRONING, IRONING...
All the singing children mime ironing or whatever the chosen action is.

WE'VE COME TO SEE POOR JENNY JONES...
The circle asks once more to see Jenny Jones but cannot see her because she is busy doing something else that they mime while singing.

WE'VE COME TO SEE POOR JENNY JONES...
The circle stands still and asks to see the child again.

YOU CAN'T SEE JENNY JONES. SHE'S SICK.
Again the parent replies.

JENNY JONES IS SICK, SICK, SICK...
The circle stands in place singing quietly while the child lies on the floor.

WE'VE COME TO SEE POOR JENNY JONES...
The circle advances and retreats quietly singing.

YOU CAN'T SEE JENNY JONES, SHE'S DYING.
The parent sadly replies.

JENNY JONES IS DYING...
The circle stands still and sings even more quietly.

WE'VE COME TO SEE POOR JENNY JONES...
The circle advances and retreats very, very quietly.

YOU CAN'T SEE JENNY JONES, SHE'S DEAD.
The parent speaks.

JENNY JONES IS DEAD...
The circle stands still and sings at a whisper.

WHAT SHALL WE DRESS HER IN? DRESS HER IN RED.
The circle sings this question three times with renewed voices and the response once.

RED IS WHAT THE SOLDIERS WEAR, SO THAT WILL NEVER DO.
The circle continues considering what color in which to dress the child.

WHAT SHALL WE DRESS HER IN? DRESS HER IN BLUE.

BLUE IS WHAT THE SAILORS WEAR, SO THAT WILL NEVER DO.

GREEN... FAIRIES
GRAY... PEOPLE
PINK... BABIES
BLACK... MOURNERS

WHITE IS WHAT THE ANGELS WEAR, SO THAT WILL DO.
A white cloth is laid over the child and the circle kneels close and weeps. Then the child leaps up and shouts, I'M ALIVE!

WE'VE COME TO SEE POOR JENNY JONES...
AND SHE'S ALIVE TODAY.
Everyone joyously advances and retreats as they hold hands in the circle and sing.

A variation for dressing the child is for the teacher to ask the children, "What shall we dress her in?" A child volunteers a color – for example, blue. The teacher asks the child, "What's blue?" "The sky." Everyone sings, BLUE IS FOR THE SKY... WE CAN'T DRESS HER IN BLUE. The teacher chooses several more children. When at last a designated child says, "White," the game proceeds as above. There are many other versions of this singing game, some of which have nothing to do with a cranky mother who keeps her daughter working when her friends ask her to play. Instead it is a suitor who is kept from seeing his lover. Poor Jenny must toil away and then dies alone. Some versions have Jenny jump up at the end dressed in white and chase the mourners!

Circle dance
Age 6 and older

SUMMER

Summer days and nights draw children outside. Dancing in sunlight and moonlight happens naturally. The levity and poise of the natural world welcomes their leaps and twirls. The finest dance floor for them is a grassy lawn, spread out under graceful trees. As the elements of air and water and the children themselves are fully liberated from their wintry confines, a new sense of musical form arises. To balance the bursting freedom, singing games enfold and order their unbounded summery mood. Like all the games that children love to play, the singing games have their own rules and boundaries that nourish their need for form.

The youngest dancers move in clumps and bunches. As guiding adults sing and lead a game, they hold them in a sunny invisible embrace. Gradually young dancers are able to come into a circle form and, by the time they are seven years old, into dynamic lines. To honor the lawfulness of child development, be considerate of the appropriateness of the dances you bring. However, as extended families gather under the summer skies, with the full spectrum of ages, the youngest ones can well be carried along in dance forms that are more oriented toward older children. The main thing is that the children experience the community spirit that flowers as the singing games progress. Anticipation is the essence of childhood; watching and imitating, even awkwardly and playfully, ensures everyone will someday be able to accomplish those steps.

If you are planning to include singing games in a gathering, begin with a circle dance, such as *Floating Down the River*. Choose a dance, like this one, where everyone is immediately involved. Within the context of the dance, they have an opportunity to connect with new friends as the circle grows. Experience has taught me that alternating between a small group of four, as in *Draw Me a Bucket of Water* and large groups, as in *Cape Cod Girls*, provides a wholesome balance. Also consider including in your summer celebrations a blend of circle and line dances with themes of your choice, as well as singing games just for the very young.

Draw Me a Bucket of Water

Draw me a buck-et of wa - ter, For my old-est daugh-ter. We got

1. none in the bunch, We're all out the bunch. You go un - der, sis-ter Sal - ly.
2. one   and   three
3. two   and   two
4. three   and   one

Frog   in   the   buck - et   and   I   can't   get   him   out.   Frog   in   the   buck - et   and   I

can't   get   him   out.   Frog   in   the   buck - et   and   I   can't   get   him   out.

1
Frog   in   the   buck - et   and   I   can't   get   him   out.

2
Frog   in   the   buck - et   and   I   can't   get   him   out.

Draw Me a Bucket of Water, written and adapted by Bessie Jones
Collected and edited by Alan Lomax
TRO–© Copyright 1972 (Renewed) Ludlow Music, Inc., New York, NY
Used by permission

Songs are carried like seeds in the craws of seabirds. This song flew across the wide ocean from England to the Georgia Sea Islands off the coast of North Carolina. Bessie Jones collected this unique version of Draw Me A Bucket Of Water in her invaluable collection of singing games called Step it Down. *Although the words have a distinct Afro-American flavor, the dance follows exactly the pattern of its British relatives. Four dancers in each set are needed to begin the dance. Everyone sings:*

DRAW ME A BUCKET OF WATER,
FOR MY OLDEST DAUGHTER.
WE GOT NONE IN THE BUNCH,
WE'RE ALL OUT THE BUNCH.
YOU GO UNDER, SISTER SALLY.

The four children form a square with their hands joined across. They seesaw back and forth in place. On the last line, the pair whose hands are on top lift one pair of clasped hands over and behind the dancer between them. Continue this pattern with each verse until all four children are in the "bunch," with their arms entwined behind them.

DRAW ME A BUCKET OF WATER,
FOR MY OLDEST DAUGHTER.
WE GOT ONE IN THE BUNCH,
AND THREE OUT THE BUNCH.
YOU GO UNDER SISTER SALLY.

The bunch now has two inside and two outside.

DRAW ME A BUCKET OF WATER,
FOR MY OLDEST DAUGHTER.
YOU GOT TWO IN THE BUNCH,
YOU GOT TWO OUT THE BUNCH.
YOU GO UNDER, SISTER SALLY.

The bunch now has three inside and one outside.

DRAW ME A BUCKET OF WATER,
FOR MY OLDEST DAUGHTER.
WE GOT THREE IN THE BUNCH,
AND ONE OUT THE BUNCH.
YOU GO UNDER, SISTER SALLY.

The bunch now has four inside with their arms woven into a basket pattern.

FROG IN THE BUCKET AND I CAN'T GET HIM OUT.
FROG IN THE BUCKET AND I CAN'T GET HIM OUT.
FROG IN THE BUCKET AND I CAN'T GET HIM OUT.
FROG IN THE BUCKET AND I CAN'T GET HIM OUT.

The dancers place right foot in the middle and use their left foot to pivot. They lean back and dance around faster and faster.

Bessie Jones has combined these two traditional dances in honor of the frogs and other creatures that used to be hauled up from the drinking well in their buckets!

Circle dance for groups of four
Age 7 and older

My Pigeon House

My pi-geon house I o-pen wide and set all my pi-geons

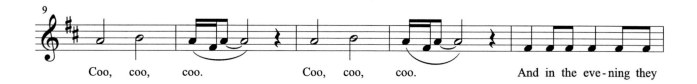

free. They fly a-round on eve-ry side and perch on the high-est tree.

Coo, coo, coo.   Coo, coo, coo.   And in the eve-ning they

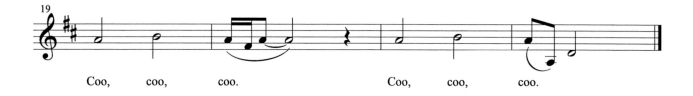

come back home and close their eyes and sleep.   Coo, coo, coo.

Coo, coo, coo.   Coo, coo, coo.

Melody by Peter Patterson, lyrics adapted from German
Music reproduced with the kind permission of Peter Patterson
and Wynstones Press.

Especially when the school year calls for closure and celebration, this singing game serves well. In kindergarten we prepare for the last day of school when the birds will "fly" by learning this song.

When the day finally arrives, everyone wears white. We perform our favorite singing games with our parents, including this one, and then release a small flock of homing pigeons. After the pigeons have circled and flown on, the teacher stands at the gate and waves goodbye to the children and their families. To begin this helpful singing game, the children stand in a circle holding hands. Everyone sings:

MY PIGEON HOUSE I OPEN WIDE AND SET ALL MY PIGEONS FREE.
Several children are chosen to be "pigeons" and stand in the middle of the circle. On OPEN, the circle children raise their arms to make window arches, and the pigeons fly under them...

THEY FLY AROUND ON EVERY SIDE
—and around the room or garden.

AND PERCH ON THE HIGHEST TREE.
COO, COO, COO. COO, COO, COO.
Each pigeon child finds a place to stand on, such as a table, a chair, a stump, or a rock.

AND IN THE EVENING THEY COME BACK HOME
The pigeons fly back through the arches...

AND CLOSE THEIR EYES AND SLEEP.
COO, COO, COO. COO, COO, COO. COO, COO, COO.
—and tuck their heads under their wing arms.

Instead of one large pigeon house, two or three people holding hands together can make little dovecotes with just one or two pigeons living in each. For very young children, the pigeon house can be made by all the adults who are present holding hands in a circle. The littlest pigeon children are safe inside.

Circle game
Age 4 and older

Cape Cod Girls

VERSE D

Cape Cod girls they have no combs. Heave a - way, heave a -

A   D   A   D

way.   They comb their hair with cod - fish bones, and we're bound for Aus - tral - ia.

CHORUS G   D   A   D

Heave a - way my bon - nie, bon - nie boys, Heave a - way, heave a - way.

G   D   A   D

Heave a - way now, don't you make a noise, and we're bound for Aus - tral - ia.

Sea chantey

Sea chanteys and work songs carry natural rhythmic vigor and good humor. They inspire a natural sense of camaraderie and easily call for a simple and playful group movement. This song was a favorite in my class. One day this dance splashed forth from our hearty singing. To begin, the children form a seated circle and sing.

Verse:

CAPE COD GIRLS THEY HAVE NO COMBS.
HEAVE AWAY, HEAVE AWAY.
THEY COMB THEIR HAIR WITH CODFISH BONES,
AND WE'RE BOUND FOR AUSTRALIA.

They slap their thighs ("patch") and clap their hands to the rhythm of the song as they sing the first verse and all the other verses.

Chorus:

HEAVE AWAY MY BONNIE, BONNIE BOYS,
HEAVE AWAY, HEAVE AWAY.
HEAVE AWAY NOW, DON'T YOU MAKE A NOISE,
AND WE'RE BOUND FOR AUSTRALIA.

On the chorus, children are chosen by the colors they are wearing, their ages, or some other distinguishing characteristic, to stand up and skip around the outside of the circle. They return back to place as they sing the word AUSTRALIA.

CAPE COD BOYS THEY HAVE NO SLEDS...
THEY SLIDE DOWN HILLS ON CODFISH HEADS...

CAPE COD CATS THEY DON'T HAVE TAILS...
THEY GOT BLOWN OFF IN SOUTHEAST GALES...

CAPE COD DOGS THEY DON'T HAVE TAILS...
THEY GOT BIT A-CHASING WHALES...

CAPE COD DOCTORS DON'T HAVE PILLS...
THEY GIVE THEIR PATIENTS CODFISH GILLS...

CAPE COD BAKERS DON'T MAKE PIES...
THEY GIVE THEIR CUSTOMERS CODFISH EYES...

Circle dance
Age 6 and older

We're Floating Down the River

We're float-ing down the ri-ver. We're float-ing down be-

low. We're float-ing down the ri-ver on the O-hi-o. There's

One in the mid-dle and you can't jump Jo-sie. One in the mid-dle and you can't jump Jo-sie.

One in the mid-dle and you can't jump Jo-sie, Oh, Miss Su-sie Brown.

American

This game from the southern United States begins with one dancer in the middle and builds up gradually to include everyone in the middle. With a very large group of thirty or more participants, try starting out with two or more in the middle to hasten the "snowballing" effect. It can be an empowering experience for shy children to be in the middle, choosing again and again others to join the growing inner circle. To begin, dancers encircle the chosen child with joined hands moving to the left. Everyone sings:

WE'RE FLOATING DOWN THE RIVER.
WE'RE FLOATING DOWN BELOW.
WE'RE FLOATING DOWN THE RIVER ON THE O-HI-O.
The children circle to the left walking at a gentle pace, one step per beat.

THERE'S ONE IN THE MIDDLE AND YOU CAN'T JUMP JOSIE.
ONE IN THE MIDDLE AND YOU CAN'T JUMP JOSIE.
ONE IN THE MIDDLE AND YOU CAN'T JUMP JOSIE,
OH, MISS SUSIE BROWN.
The chosen child in the middle dances or skips around the inside of the circle while the children in the circle tap their toes and clap their hands to accompany the dancing. After the last line, the child chooses a partner to bring into the inner circle.

WE'RE FLOATING DOWN THE RIVER...
The two children in the middle circle to the right and the outer circle circles left.

TWO IN THE MIDDLE AND YOU CAN'T JUMP JOSIE...
Two children dance around together or separately inside the circle while the outside circle taps their toes and claps. At the end, both children choose new partners and get ready to circle right.

The gently paced chorus is followed each time by the lively dancing as the inner circle grows larger:

FOUR IN THE MIDDLE...
EIGHT...
SIXTEEN...
When everyone is chosen and the outer circle has become the inner circle, remember to circle right on the chorus! Then the final verse is

WE'RE ALL IN THE MIDDLE...

Circle dance
Age 6 and older

circle dances

The circle is a powerful, yet comforting form—the shape of a nest, a tepee, and a hug. Standing next to one another, the dancers are equally distant from the center. Yet it is not easy for young children to form a circle. They are much more inclined to bunch together like grapes. In kindergarten, I invite the children into "a golden ring" by singing, "Gather together, in a circle we will sing. Gather together, we will make a golden ring." Children love to hear everyday ho-hum directions dressed up in descriptive language full of images that bring light and perhaps also a touch of humor to the ordinary. "Get in a circle" is quite a different invitation from, "The ring is calling to you."

The circle serves many kinds of dances. The dancers can remain in one place, as in *I Will Pass the Shoe*, or move to the left, clockwise. Sometimes the action of the singing game takes place in a little vignette inside the circle, as in *Brown Girl*, or outside the circle, as in *Charlie*. Chosen players can pass through archways formed by the standing circle, as in *Shoo-Fly*, or a circle can be "broken" and turn into a spiral, like *Stoopin' On the Window*.

Within the embrace of the circle, through rhythmic movements and patterns, children build a sense of security and success. They are able to develop coordination and grace. Much skill is involved in walking around the circle, first in front of one child, and behind the next, then in front and behind, until all have returned to the starting point. This is called "weaving," a pattern that appears in many singing games, such as *Go Round and Round the Village*. Over a period of weeks or months, the children's confidence blossoms as they learn and practice new songs and dances that incorporate such familiar patterns.

When I begin teaching the "weaving" pattern, which is also found in *Bonnie Bluebells*, I first take one child by the hand and weave in and out around a circle of children quietly seated with legs crossed in front of them. I might extend the imagination, by saying, "Now the bluebells are standing up together. Let's join hands and make a beautiful meadow of bluebells." Soon we are ready to play the game with children weaving in and out among the "Bonnie Bluebells" on their own.

A weaving pattern leads naturally to other forms. Sometimes the children and I draw on a piece of paper what we have been dancing. I might draw little dots seated in a circle. Then with another color, I might draw a continuous line weaving in and out, just as we have done during the dance.

Singing games provide a wide spectrum of physical exercises that must be presented in a logical developmentally-appropriate sequence, from simple to complex. They are a way to be in tune with one's body and its unique geography, as well as being aware of surrounding space and its occupants.

Partner dances grow naturally out of circle dances. Two people join hands to form their own little circle. To introduce a partner dance, such as *Brother, Come and Dance with Me*, first dance the game with the whole group. Once the tune and actions are secure, I say "Turn to the friend next to you," or I go around the circle pairing the children off, saying, " Here are two friends." Even dancing with a doll or stuffed animal or with Mr. Nobody can be fun.

To pair up in large circles, try the domino technique, something I learned from Peter and Mary Alice Amidon of Vermont. The first two people in the circle turn toward each other as partners, followed immediately by the next two, and the next two, and so on. Enjoy!

I Will Pass the Shoe

American

Children love and need ceremonious patterns. Ordinary and necessary objects, such as shoes, come with their set of laws. For instance, shoes come in pairs. They must be laced and unlaced, fastened and unfastened, polished and washed, kept together, and given to someone else when they no longer fit. This song supports every child's need for orderly having and giving. To begin, the children take off their shoes and sit in a circle.

I WILL PASS THE SHOE FROM ME TO YOU, TO YOU.
YOU PASS THE SHOE...
Placing their shoes in front of them, they pass both shoes, in rhythm with the music, to their neighbor on the right. Each pair of shoes passes around the circle.

AND DO JUST WHAT I DO.
Holding a pair of shoes, the children move the shoes toward the neighbor on their right on DO. Then they move to the neighbor on their left on WHAT, and then back in front of themselves on the second DO. They continue singing the song again as they pass that pair of shoes to their neighbor on the right.

One shoe, or pair of shoes, can be passed when the children are first learning. I sing this song to help establish an orderly rhythm when passing out beanbags or rhythm sticks for math or other lessons.

Circle game
Age 6 and older

Old King Glory of the Mountain

Old King Glo - ry of the moun - tain, The moun - tain rose so high, It rose up to the sky and it's one, two, three fol - low me.

American

Singing Games

Every child needs the experience of being lifted up to royal stature. Truly noble kings and queens, princesses and princes are necessary archetypes to experience in children's play. The magnificent words of this song match the dignifying rhythm of the melody. To begin, the children stand in a circle, and join hands. Everyone sings:

OLD KING GLORY OF THE MOUNTAIN,
One child is chosen to walk around the outside of the circle.

THE MOUNTAIN ROSE SO HIGH, IT ROSE UP TO THE SKY
The children in the circle take one step in and raise their hands up, and then lower them.

AND IT'S ONE, TWO, THREE FOLLOW ME.
The child circling the outside taps three consecutive children on the shoulder. Those four children join hands and walk around the outside of the circle together as the game begins again. The lead child continues to tap three children on ONE, TWO THREE. Finally, all the children have joined the new line, creating a new circle.

Said at the very end:
AND WE'LL ALL BOW DOWN TO THE MOUNTAIN.
Everyone stands still and bows to the center of the circle. If you are playing with a small group, ask the third child tapped to join the line.

Circle game
Age 6 and older

Oh, How Lovely is the Evening

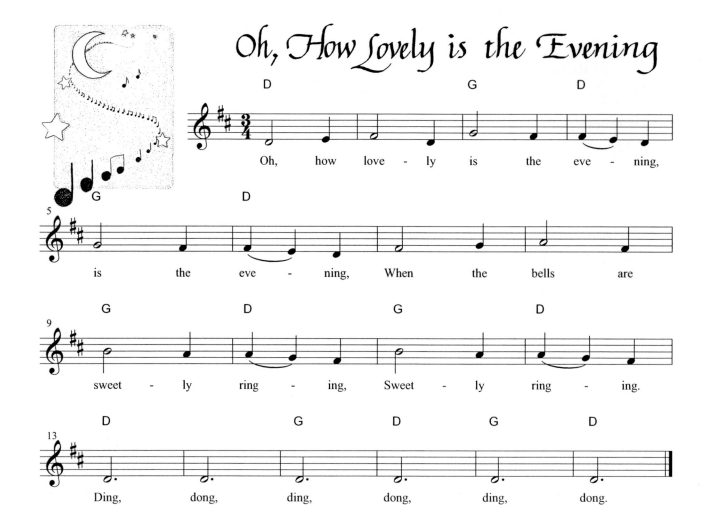

German

On a long car trip to a conference, the idea for this dance came to mind. I was looking for a singing game for adults who would be spending a long, productive day together. I wanted a song that everyone would already know, or could easily learn, and out of that to create a dance. Because OH, HOW LOVELY IS THE EVENING was familiar and the steps simple, and because it is a round, this singing game brought a special sense of peace and closure to the whole group. I recommend that everyone sing and dance the entire song several times, before designating groups for the different voices of the round. To begin, all the dancers stand in a circle and everyone sings:

OH, HOW LOVELY IS THE EVENING, IS THE EVENING,
Everyone takes six steps toward the center of the circle.

WHEN THE BELLS ARE SWEETLY RINGING, SWEETLY RINGING.
Everyone joins hands and holds them high to make arches.

DING, DONG, DING, DONG, DING, DONG.
Everyone drops hands and takes six steps back to the circle.

To dance the round, have the participants number off 1, 2, or 3 around the circle. Each group takes turns performing the entire dance alone, while the others watch and sing along. When everyone has practiced, the final step is to perform the dance as a round.

The 1s begin by walking in six steps as they sing the first line of the song. As they join hands and make a circle of arches and begin singing the second verse, the 2s start walking in. They stoop under the arches of the 1s, who start walking backwards to place. At the same time, the 3s are walking forward, and the 2s are making the arches. The song continues until each group returns to the circle. The dance ends on the last chorus of DING, DONG, DING, DONG.

A simpler variation for a large group is to form three concentric circles. The dance is simply done by joining hands and circling left on the first line and then to the right on the second line. On the third line the dancers stand in place and swing their joined arms in time to the chiming bells. To dance as a round, the smallest inside circle begins by singing and moving to the left. As they move to the right on the second line, the middle circle begins singing the first line and moving left. When the smallest circle is swinging their arms for the final line, the middle circle is moving to the right and the outside circle begins moving to the left. On the third time through the round, each circle continues to sing the final line until all the dancers are swinging their arms and singing: DING, DONG, DING, DONG, DING, DONG. This variation works well with a mixed age group of young and old dancing together.

WHEN THE SILVER BELLS ARE RINGING can be used as alternate words for the second line.

Circle dance
First variation: Age 12 and older
Second variation: Mixed age group

Go 'Round and 'Round the Village

Go 'round and 'round the vil - lage, Go 'round and 'round the
Go in and out the win - dow, Go in and out the

vil - lage, Go 'round and 'round the vil - lage, As we have done be - fore.
win - dow, Go in and out the win - dow, As we have done be - fore.

English

ALTERNATE MELODY

'Round and 'round the vil - lage, 'Round and 'round the vil - lage,

'Round and 'round the vil - lage, As we have done be - fore.

Singing Games

According to Alice B. Gomme, whose fascinating book, The Traditional Games of England, Scotland and Ireland, *was published in 1894, this is a custom game in which the children re-enact adult proprieties. In this case, they act as a chorus in the classical Greek theater tradition. Their song narrates a sequence of events that has been recounted over and over again, which is suggested by the refrain, AS WE HAVE DONE BEFORE. To begin, the children stand in a circle. As they sing, they move to the left which in Celtic lore is called "sun-wise."*

GO 'ROUND AND 'ROUND THE VILLAGE,
GO 'ROUND AND 'ROUND THE VILLAGE,
GO 'ROUND AND 'ROUND THE VILLAGE,
AS WE HAVE DONE BEFORE.

The children continue circling "sun-wise" as one child walks around the outside of the circle.

GO IN AND OUT THE WINDOWS,
GO IN AND OUT THE WINDOWS,
GO IN AND OUT THE WINDOWS,
AS WE HAVE DONE BEFORE.

The "village children" with joined hands raise them to form window arches. The moving child weaves in and out through the windows around the circle.

STAND AND FACE YOUR PARTNER.

This verse is repeated three times as the "village children" drop their hands and stand still. The moving child stands in front of another child in the village circle.

FOLLOW ME TO LONDON.

Again, this verse is repeated three times as the "village children" remain standing and the moving child and the chosen partner walk around the outside of the circle.

SHAKE HANDS WITH YOUR PARTNER.

As this verse is repeated three times, the child and partner shake hands. The first child returns to the circle, while the partner becomes the new moving child.

There are many variations of this singing game popular in both England and America. Mrs. Gomme herself collected nineteen versions! Here are some examples: GO ROUND AND ROUND THE VALLEY... NOW FOLLOW ME TO BOSTON... CHASE HER BACK TO SCOTLAND... TAKE HER OFF TO LONDON... KISS HER BEFORE YOU LEAVE HER...

Circle game
Age 7 and older

Circle Dances

Charlie Over the Ocean

LEADER G   GROUP

Char-lie ov-er the o-cean, Char-lie o-ver the o-cean,

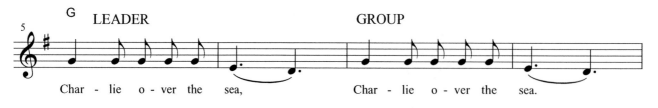

G LEADER   GROUP

Char-lie o-ver the sea, Char-lie o-ver the sea.

G LEADER   GROUP

Char-lie caught a black-bird, Char-lie caught a black-bird,

G LEADER   GROUP

Can't catch me, Can't catch me.

American

When children need to run and chase, this is the game for them! During inclement weather, this singing game has satisfied even the liveliest players. It goes quickly, so many can have a turn at the chase. To begin, the children join hands and circle to the left. Someone is chosen to be "Charlie," who walks around the outside of the circle to the right. This is a "call and response" song. The leader can be the teacher or another child.

Leader: **CHARLIE OVER THE OCEAN,**

Group: **CHARLIE OVER THE OCEAN,**

Leader: **CHARLIE OVER THE SEA,**

Group: **CHARLIE OVER THE SEA.**

Leader: **CHARLIE CAUGHT A BLACKBIRD,**

Group: **CHARLIE CAUGHT A BLACKBIRD,**

Leader: **CAN'T CATCH ME,**

Group: **CAN'T CATCH ME.**

On the last ME, Charlie tags another child and runs around the circle back to that child's place with the tagged child in pursuit. In our class it does not matter who arrives first. The old Charlie joins the circle, while the tagged child becomes the new Charlie.

Circle dance
Age 7 and older

Brown Girl

There's a brown girl in the ring, tra la la la la. There's a brown girl in the ring, tra la la la la la. Brown girl in the ring, tra la la la la. And she looks like the su-gar in the plum, plum, plum.

VERSE

Show me a mo-tion, tra la la la la. Show me a mo-tion, tra la la la la la. Show me a mo-tion, tra la la la la. And she looks like the su-gar in the plum, plum, plum.

Jamaican

This is an energetic game from the West Indies, which is enjoyed by children and adults. It provides an opportunity to show off, and never fails to produce lots of laughter, especially when the adults are chosen to be in the middle. Make sure that the syncopated rhythm of the PLUM, PLUM, PLUM is exact. It adds to the spice and upbeat mood. To begin, dancers form a circle, holding hands. Someone is chosen to be in the middle, as the others begin to sing and circle to the left.

Introduction:
THERE'S A BROWN GIRL IN THE RING, TRA LA LA LA LA.
THERE'S A BROWN GIRL IN THE RING, TRA LA LA LA LA LA.
BROWN GIRL IN THE RING, TRA LA LA LA LA.
AND SHE LOOKS LIKE THE SUGAR IN THE PLUM, PLUM , PLUM.
The child in the middle stands still or dances freely, while the other children circle around her.

Verse one:
SHOW ME A MOTION, TRA LA LA LA LA.
SHOW ME A MOTION, TRA LA LA LA LA LA.
SHOW ME A MOTION, TRA LA LA LA LA.
AND SHE LOOKS LIKE THE SUGAR IN THE PLUM, PLUM, PLUM.
The child in the middle performs an action (clapping, jumping, twirling, etc.) and the circle children imitate her.

Verse two:
SKIP ACROSS THE OCEAN, TRA LA LA LA LA,
SKIP ACROSS THE OCEAN, TRA LA LA LA LA LA.
SKIP ACROSS THE OCEAN, TRA LA LA LA LA,
AND SHE LOOKS LIKE THE SUGAR IN THE PLUM, PLUM, PLUM.
The child in the middle skips around the outside of the circle, as space permits. When the singing is over a new child is chosen, and the game repeats.

Often children choose stunts, such as cartwheels and somersaults, to challenge their friends.

Circle game
Age 7 and older

Brother Come and Dance

Broth-er, come and dance with me. Both my hands I off-er thee.

Right foot first, left foot then, Round a-bout and back a-gain.

With your foot you tap, tap, tap. With your hands you clap, clap, clap.
With your head you nick, nick, nick. With your fingers you click, click, click.

Right foot first, left foot then, Round a-bout and back a-gain. back a-gain. Oh,

tra la la la la la la la la. Oh, tra la la la la la la la. Oh, la.

German

This folk dance is from Hansel and Gretel, *an operetta created by Engelbert Humperdinck based upon the Grimms' fairy tale of the same name. Humperdinck wove familiar folk tunes and songs into the story lines. Unlike the Grimms' version, the operatic witch is baked into gingerbread and the children are happily reunited with their parents at the end. It is the tradition in our kindergarten each year at Halloween to perform a simplified version of the play with some of the songs. One of our favorites is the following partner dance:*

BROTHER, COME AND DANCE WITH ME. BOTH MY HANDS I OFFER THEE.
Partners face each other and offer their hands to one another.

RIGHT FOOT FIRST, LEFT FOOT THEN,
All point their right foot, then their left foot.

ROUND ABOUT AND BACK AGAIN.
Partners hold hands and circle once around.

WITH YOUR FOOT YOU TAP, TAP, TAP.
WITH YOUR HANDS YOU CLAP, CLAP, CLAP.
All tap their feet and then clap their hands.

RIGHT FOOT FIRST, LEFT FOOT THEN,
All point their right foot, then their left foot.

ROUND ABOUT AND BACK AGAIN.
Partners hold hands and circle once around.

WITH YOUR HEAD YOU NICK, NICK, NICK.
All move their heads from side to side.

WITH YOUR FINGERS YOU CLICK, CLICK, CLICK.
All snap their fingers.

RIGHT FOOT FIRST, LEFT FOOT THEN, ROUND ABOUT AND BACK AGAIN.
Everyone points right foot then left foot and turns around with partner.

OH, TRA LA LA LA LA LA LA LA LA OH, TRA LA LA LA LA LA LA.
OH, TRA LA LA LA LA LA LA LA LA OH, TRA LA LA LA LA LA LA.
Partners hold hands and turn around together.

A variation for older dancers, especially adults, is to do the Grand Right and Left during the TRA LA LAs. Partners face one another and take left hands. All extend their right hands to their partners, and then reach out with left hands to the person coming towards them. They pull that person by as they stretch out their left hands to the next person. The dancers always continue in the same direction following the same person in front of them, greeting new partners coming from the opposite direction. They alternate left hands and right hands until the TRA LA LAs are finished, and then begin the dance again with a new partner. A variation for the youngest dancers is for the children to start in a standing circle, and stay in the circle throughout the song, moving together on the TRA LA LAs.

Circle or partner dance
Age 6 and older

Billy Boy

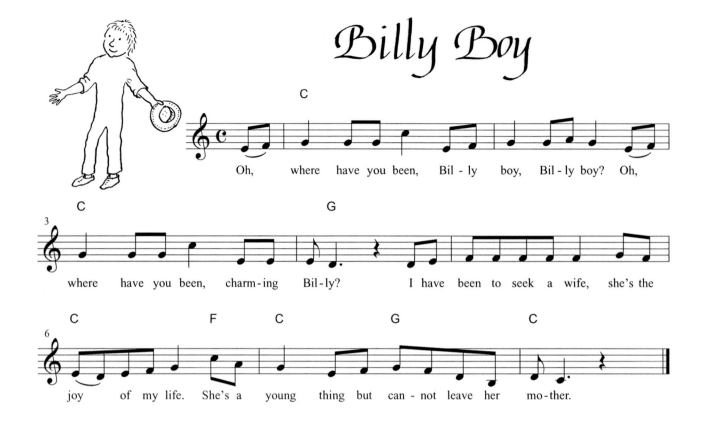

American

This is an example an of old American folk song that inspired me one day to make up a dance for the children. Perhaps you have a favorite song from your childhood that could become a dance. Here the children stand in a circle and face into the middle to start.

OH, WHERE HAVE YOU BEEN, BIILY BOY, BILLY BOY?
The dancers extend their right foot. Then they put their feet together and extend the left foot and put their feet together.

OH, WHERE HAVE YOU BEEN, CHARMING BILLY?
The children repeat the above steps.

I HAVE BEEN TO SEEK A WIFE,
With both hands, all the children slap their thighs, which is called "patching," and then clap hands.

SHE'S THE JOY OF MY LIFE.
The children hold palms up facing toward the middle of the circle and then clap hands together.

SHE'S A YOUNG THING BUT CANNOT LEAVE HER MOTHER.
Each child turns around in place.

Additional verses:

CAN SHE BAKE A CHERRY PIE, BILLY BOY, BILLY BOY?
CAN SHE BAKE A CHERRY PIE, CHARMING BILLY?
SHE CAN BAKE A CHERRY PIE, QUICK AS A CAT CAN WINK ITS EYE.
SHE'S A YOUNG THING AND CANNOT LEAVE HER MOTHER.

DID SHE TAKE YOUR COAT, BILLY BOY, BILLY BOY?...
YES, SHE TOOK MY COAT AND SHE FED IT TO THE GOAT...

DID SHE OFFER YOU A CHAIR, BILLY BOY, BILLY BOY?...
YES, SHE OFFERED ME A CHAIR, BUT THE BOTTOM WASN'T THERE...

HOW OLD IS SHE, BILLY BOY, BILLY BOY?...
SHE IS 20 AND 11, 2 TIMES 6 AND 4 TIMES 7...

This song lends itself to endless silly verses you can make up with the children, as we did.

DID SHE TAKE YOUR HAT?...
YES, SHE TOOK MY HAT AND SHE FED IT TO THE CAT...

DID SHE TAKE YOUR SOCKS?...
YES, SHE TOOK MY SOCKS AND SHE FED THEM TO THE FOX...

Try this dance as a partner dance. Each child faces a partner and performs the dance as above. On SHE'S THE JOY the partners clap hands together and then clap their own hands. The partners join hands and circle around on SHE'S A YOUNG THING. After finishing one verse, everyone can also turn around to face a new partner and begin again.

A variation for older children is for them to stand in a circle and face their partners. For the first two lines, OH, WHERE HAVE YOU BEEN, BILLY BOY...the children do a Grand Right and Left. All extend their right hands to their partners, and then reach out with left hands to the person coming towards them. Always proceeding in the same direction, alternating right and left hands, dancers continue in this Grand Right and Left around the circle Everyone stops and faces a new partner for the patch, clap, clap, clap on I HAVE BEEN TO SEEK.... The new partners join hands and turn around in a circle on SHE'S A YOUNG THING. Everyone gets ready for the Grand Right and Left on the next verse. Older children will enjoy adding fancy clapping patterns, such as clapping twice as fast, or "double time," with their partners.

Circle or partner dance
Age 7 and older

Stoopin' on the Window

Stoop-in' on the win-dow, wind the ball.

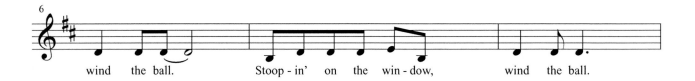

Stoop-in' on the win-dow, wind the ball. Stoop-in' on the win-dow,

wind the ball. Stoop-in' on the win-dow, wind the ball.

REPEAT MANY TIMES

Let's wind the ball, a - gain, a - gain, a - gain.

REPEAT MANY TIMES

Un - wind the ball, a - gain, a - gain, a - gain.

African American

136   Singing Games

This spiral dance is based on an American "call and response" song. Although the origin of the words is unknown, it is great fun to dance and speculate on their meaning. To begin, the dancers form a line and join hands. The leader begins to sing and wind the line into a spiral.

The call by the leader:
STOOPIN' ON THE WINDOW,
The response by the dancers:
WIND THE BALL.
Leader:
STOOPIN' ON THE WINDOW,
Dancers:
WIND THE BALL.
Leader:
STOOPIN' ON THE WINDOW,
Dancers:
WIND THE BALL.
Leader:
STOOPIN' ON THE WINDOW,
Dancers:
WIND THE BALL.

Leader:
LET'S WIND THE BALL,
The leader continues to wind the spiral tighter and tighter.
Dancers:
AGAIN, AGAIN, AGAIN.
The dancers respond as they follow the leader.
Leader:
LET'S WIND THE BALL,
Dancers:
AGAIN, AGAIN, AGAIN.
Leader:
UNWIND THE BALL,
The leader begins to unwind the spiral by reversing the direction without skipping a beat, unlike *Wind Up the Apple Tree*, where the spiral stops before unwinding.
Dancers:
AGAIN, AGAIN, AGAIN.
The dancers follow.
Leader:
UNWIND THE BALL,
Dancer:
AGAIN, AGAIN, AGAIN.

Spiral line dance
Age 7 and older

Shoo, Fly

Shoo, fly, don't bo - ther me. Shoo, fly, don't bo - ther me.

Shoo, fly, don't bot - ther me for I be - long to some - bo - dy. I

feel, I feel, I feel like a morn - ing star. I

feel, I feel, I feel like a morn - ing star.

American

This singing game gives a picture of a healthy life and a well-functioning immune system. What could be more empowering than to be able to protect our personal space and to shine like a morning star? Originally from the Civil War period, this American singing game is a great way to start a community gathering and to develop group spirit. To begin, all the dancers join hands together in a circle and sing.

SHOO, FLY, DON'T BOTHER ME.
The dancers take four steps toward the center of the circle.

SHOO, FLY, DON'T BOTHER ME.
They take four steps backward to the original circle.

SHOO, FLY, DON'T BOTHER ME
Again, they take four steps toward the center...

FOR I BELONG TO SOMEBODY.
...and take four steps back to the original circle.

I FEEL, I FEEL, I FEEL LIKE A MORNING STAR.
I FEEL, I FEEL, I FEEL LIKE A MORNING STAR.
The leader drops hands with the person on the right. Everyone else keeps holding hands. The person to the right and her neighbor to the right raise joined hands to form an archway. The leader bends under the arch, pulling along the line of dancers and bending to the left as she emerges and continues curving toward the left, until a new circle has been formed. The dancers who form the arch twist under to rejoin the circle without letting go of hands. The whole group keeps singing I FEEL LIKE A MORNING STAR, until everyone is through the arch and has returned to the circle. The song continues with a new leader.

A variation begins in the same way. On the MORNING STAR chorus, the dancers keep holding hands. Two stand opposite the leader and raise their hands to make an arch. The leader pulls her neighbors across the circle and through the arch. This time the circle will be turned inside out. They sing the song again from the beginning, but this time stepping four steps backward and then forward to form a circle. The leader walks backward through the same arch, pulling everyone with her on the MORNING STAR chorus.

A second variation begins the same way as the first one. This time, when the leader has pulled her first neighbor under the arch that has just formed on the opposite side of the circle, they immediately stop and form a second arch. Now everyone, still holding hands, passes under a double arch.

Circle dance
Age 7 and older

Rig-a-Jig-Jig

VERSE

As I was walk-ing down the street, Down the street, down the street, A

pret - ty friend I chanced to meet. Hi ho, hi ho, hi ho.

CHORUS

Rig - a jig-jig and a - way we go, A - way we go, a - way we go.

Rig - a jig-jig and a - way we go, Hi ho, hi ho, hi ho.

English

This traditional English song has a lively skipping rhythm. The joyous skill of skipping is essential to everyone's well-being. The feeling of skipping with lightness, coordination and balance has lived for generations in this captivating rhyme. To begin, the children stand in a circle and sing:

Verse:
> **AS I WAS WALKING DOWN THE STREET,**
> **DOWN THE STREET, DOWN THE STREET,**

One child is chosen to *walk* around the outside of the circle.

> **A PRETTY FRIEND I CHANCED TO MEET.**
> **HI HO, HI HO, HI HO.**

The child *walks* outside the circle and stops behind a friend.

Chorus:
> **RIG-A JIG-JIG AND AWAY WE GO,**
> **AWAY WE GO, AWAY WE GO.**
> **RIG-A JIG-JIG AND AWAY WE GO,**
> **HI-HO, HI-HO, HI-HO.**

The two children *skip* around the outside of the circle. As the song ends, the first child *skips* to place and the second child continues walking.

This game can also be played in "follow-the-leader" style, first walking and then skipping. Another variation can be played in "snowballing" style by starting with one child as before, but instead of returning to place, the two children continue. Each chooses a friend, so that now four are skipping on the RIG-A JIG-JIG chorus. The four becomes eight, and so on. This is another opportunity to include everyone. When the circle has completely dissolved, a designated leader leads the skipping line down the hall and out the door to play!

Circle or line game
Age 6 and older

American

Our present culture offers us few opportunities to bow and to curtsey. This old American game has infinite possibilities and can be as easy or as complicated as desired. Start out in a standing circle and sing, as everyone bows down three times:

BOW DOWN, OH BELINDA.
BOW DOWN, OH BELINDA.
BOW DOWN, OH BELINDA.
WON'T YOU BE MY PARTNER?

The children continue singing and perform each verse appropriately.

TOUCH THE GROUND, OH BELINDA...
TOUCH THE SKY...
TIPTOE 'ROUND...
STOMP AROUND...
CLAP YOUR HANDS...
TAP YOUR TOES...
INTO THE MIDDLE...
Everyone steps forward to the middle.
OUT TO THE SIDE...
Everyone returns to the original circle.
SIT RIGHT DOWN...
FOLLOW ME...
Continue with your own verses.

A variation of this popular folk melody is danced with partners.

RIGHT HANDS 'ROUND...
Everyone faces a partner and holding right hands walks a complete circle around one another. Holding onto one another's elbows or linking elbows is also fun.

LEFT HANDS 'ROUND...
BOTH HANDS 'ROUND...

DO-SI-DO...
This is an American version of *Dos à dos*, a French term meaning "back to back." Everyone walks around his or her partner. In order to move back to back, everyone must face forward throughout the entire maneuver.

WRING THE DISHRAG...
Partners face forward, and while holding hands up overhead, turn back to back. They keep turning in this way, "wringing the dishrag" three times.

PROMENADE...
Partners join right hands together and left hands together and walk around the circle back to their original place.

Additional verses can be made with a mathematical flavor: WITH YOUR PARTNER MAKE A CIRCLE... (SQUARE, DIAMOND, RECTANGLE) OH, BELINDA. Partners form shapes while singing by joining hands or legs and standing or lying on the floor. TWO BY TWO... Partners promenade around the circle. FOUR BY FOUR... Two couples join together to promenade around the large circle. Alternately they can join hands, form a small circle moving counterclockwise. SIX BY SIX... THREE BY THREE... Going from TWO BY TWO to THREE BY THREE is not recommended. Instead, try going from SIX BY SIX to THREE BY THREE.

Other verses can be made with an alphabetical flavor:

WITH YOUR PARTNER MAKE AN "L" (name a letter)...
Working together, partners form the letter L with their bodies.
Children and adults enjoy the challenge of forming all the letters of the alphabet and numbers, too, by working cooperatively together.

Verses can be made with a folk dance flavor.

TWO BY TWO...
Partners dance together.

FOUR BY FOUR...
Two couples join to dance in a circle.

CIRCLE 'ROUND...
The foursome circles to the left.

RIGHT HAND STAR...
The foursome puts their right hands in the middle holding on to each other's wrists to form a "star." The trick is to hold on to the wrist of your neighbor to the left.

LEFT HAND STAR...
The foursome puts their left hands into the middle of the small circle to form a "star."

CIRCLE 'ROUND...
The foursome joins hands and circles left.

THROUGH THE ARCH...
Keeping hands joined, one couple makes an arch and the other couple goes under the arch so that now the dancers are facing out, with their backs to the center.

INTO THE MIDDLE...
The foursome steps into the middle and out again.

BACK THROUGH THE ARCH...
The couples return through the arch to their original places.

CIRCLE 'ROUND...

EIGHT BY EIGHT...
One group joins another group and repeats the above pattern. Add another group on to that group and continue until everyone is included in one giant circle. End by singing BOW DOWN, OH BELINDA, and all bow together.

This version includes many elements found in traditional folk dances and serves as an entry to more complex steps and forms of American square and contra dancing. Because this dance is so adaptable, it works especially well with large groups of children or adults. I have danced it with as many as fifty children of mixed ages. On rainy days it has served as a joyful outlet.

Circle or partner dance
Mixed ages

Button

American

ALTERNATE MELODIC PHRASE

This is a rainy day game for a sitting circle of children. A button or small object is passed around the circle so that no one sees it travelling from hand to hand. A child is chosen to be the watcher. As the button passes from hand to hand, the watcher observes where it ends up. At the end of the song, the watcher has two guesses to identify who has the object.

BUTTON, YOU MUST WANDER, WANDER, WANDER.
BUTTON, YOU MUST WANDER EVERYWHERE.
BRIGHT EYES WILL FIND YOU.
SHARP EYES WILL FIND YOU.
BUTTON, YOU MUST WANDER EVERYWHERE.

A variation for young children is for a ring to be strung on a long piece of yarn. The children sitting in the circle hold onto the yarn and slide the ring from hand to hand as they sing. This is a challenging game that can engage even the most reluctant of players.

Circle game
Age 5½ and older

Line Dances

"Follow the leader" dances are a gentle transition from the comforting enclosure of a circle. *Follow My Leader to London Town* is a simple meandering line dance in which everyone imitates the movements of the leader. *The Big Ship* is an example of a single line being twisted and then untwisted. Other line dances involve "contra" lines, where two lines of children face their partners standing in the opposite line.

When I teach double line dances to school-age children, I draw on the floor to mark their places. I even tie colorful yarn around their right wrists to clarify left and right. These double line dances are best suited for children of seven years and older, for they require thoughtful attention to the movements as well as to the other players. The cooperative spirit and the challenge of the game, as in *Sandgate,* entice reluctant players. As children mature in their thinking, more complex resonances arise between music and movement. Their enjoyment of dancing in lines parallels their growing capacity to follow lines of thought. Older children and adults rally to dances that resemble conversations and debates, as in *Knots of May*.

Knowing the needs of your group and the stages of development enables you to choose the appropriate singing games for their benefit and enjoyment. Your awareness of the social dynamics in a group and the potential harmonious effect of these dances will lead you to success.

Yonder They Come

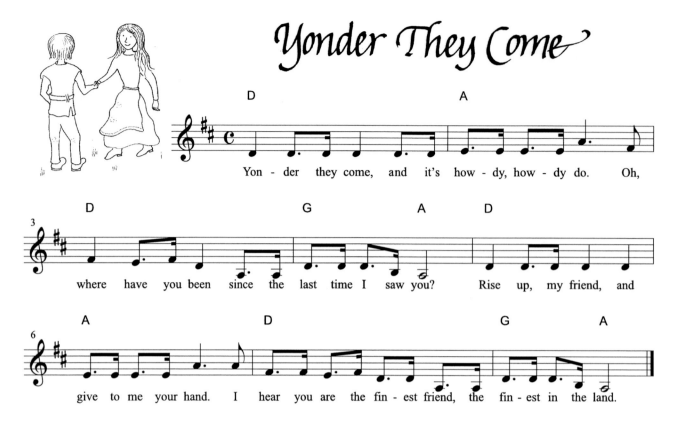

Yon-der they come, and it's how-dy, how-dy do. Oh,
where have you been since the last time I saw you? Rise up, my friend, and
give to me your hand. I hear you are the fin-est friend, the fin-est in the land.

American

After singing this song from the American South for several years in the classroom, one day I decided to turn it into a dance. Since then I have had the pleasure of sharing it with many colleagues who have included it in parent evenings and faculty meetings as a refreshing way to greet everyone present. The simplest way to introduce the song is for the leader to sing and walk around the circle, shaking hands with everyone and looking them in the eye. If the children are seated, each one stands up after shaking hands. For older children and adults, begin with all participants in a circle. Everyone sings:

YONDER THEY COME, AND IT'S HOWDY, HOWDY DO.
OH, WHERE HAVE YOU BEEN SINCE THE LAST TIME I SAW YOU?
RISE UP, MY FRIEND, AND GIVE TO ME YOUR HAND.
I HEAR YOU ARE THE FINEST FRIEND, THE FINEST IN THE LAND.

Consider each person A,B,C,D. . . . as they stand in the circle. The leader turns and shakes hands with A, and then goes on to shake hands with B. When the leader reaches C, A follows the leader and shakes hands with B. When the leader reaches D, A shakes C, B stands ready. When the leader reaches E, A shakes D, B shakes C. When the leader reaches F, A shakes hands with E, B shakes hands with D, and C stands ready, and so on, moving consecutively around the circle. This pattern can continue until the leader reaches the last person. It is not as complicated as it sounds!

Circle and line dance
Age 9 and older.

Singing Games

Follow My Leader

Fol-low my lead-er to Lon-don town, Lon-don town, Lon-don town.

Fol-low my lead-er to Lon-don town, so ear-ly in the morn-ing.

English

On the grand tour of life, our feet carry us from place to place. In this traditional English rhyme, the journey requires many different kinds of steps, and like all good leaders, the leader of this dance makes it possible for all the followers to enjoy the journey. To begin, for the youngest travelers, make a circle. Everyone sings:

**FOLLOW MY LEADER TO LONDON TOWN,
LONDON TOWN, LONDON TOWN.
FOLLOW MY LEADER TO LONDON TOWN,
SO EARLY IN THE MORNING.**
The children walk around the circle to the left.

**GALLOPING HORSES TO LONDON TOWN...
SKIPPING ALONG...
HOPPING ALONG...
STOMPING ALONG...
WALKING QUIETLY...
TIPTOEING ALONG...
SKATING ALONG...
CRAWLING ALONG...
DANCING ALONG...
SITTING DOWN IN LONDON TOWN...**
The children mime each verse appropriately as they continue moving to the left in their circle. For children seven and older, choose a leader. Everyone follows the leader around the room, singing and miming the above verses.

After one verse, the leader goes to the end of the line and the next child assumes the role of leader. This song easily invites improvisations. For instance, on the words DON-KEY AND CART TO LONDON TOWN, groups of three can travel together, one child as the donkey leading two children in the cart.

Circle or line dance
Age 6 and older

The Big Ship

The big ship sails through the al-ley, al-ley-o, the al-ley, al-ley-o, the al-ley, al-ley-o. The big ship sails through the al-ley, al-ley-o, on the last day of Sep-tem-ber.

English

A single line is versatile. It can be moved by following a leader. It can be straight, or curved into endless forms. In this English nautical dance, the dancers twist into a knotted line. The game requires six or more dancers, who begin by holding hands in a line. A child at one end, the head dancer, places her free hand on something stationary that can act as an anchor, such as a wall, a post, or a tree. This forms an archway. The child at the opposite end of the line is "the tail."

**THE BIG SHIP SAILS THROUGH THE ALLEY, ALLEY-O,
THE ALLEY, ALLEY-O, THE ALLEY, ALLEY-O.
THE BIG SHIP SAILS THROUGH THE ALLEY, ALLEY-O,
ON THE LAST DAY OF SEPTEMBER.**

The tail leads the line under the arch formed by the head dancer and the wall. Instead of ducking under the arch after the tail, the head dancer twists only halfway, ending up with arms crossed in front. Meanwhile the tail is now walking back towards the arch made by the head dancer and her neighbor. This time, the neighbor twists around, not going under the arch, and ends up with arms crossed in front. The tail continues to lead the line between each successive child, until all are neatly twisted, with their arms crossed in front of them.

**WE'LL DIP OUR HEADS IN THE DEEP BLUE SEA,
THE DEEP BLUE SEA, THE DEEP BLUE SEA.
WE'LL DIP OUR HEADS IN THE DEEP BLUE SEA,
ON THE LAST DAY OF SEPTEMBER.**

The head and the tail join hands, still crossed, to form a circle. Stepping to the left, the circle of children bob down and up on the word DIP by slightly bending their knees.

**THE CAPTAIN SAID, "THIS WILL NEVER, NEVER DO,
NEVER, NEVER DO, NEVER, NEVER DO."
THE CAPTAIN SAID, "THIS WILL NEVER, NEVER DO,
ON THE LAST DAY OF SEPTEMBER."**

The children let go of hands and wave their pointer fingers at one another.

The Big Ship is based on the old street game of *Thread the Needle*, which is a line that requires lots of space. The head is now called "the eye of the needle" and the tail is "the thread." The thread runs as fast as possible, pulling the line of at least six children who are holding hands along with her under the arch formed by the eye and his neighbor. When everyone has been pulled through, the roles are immediately reversed and the former eye dashes off for the arch made by the new eye and neighbor. This game moves very fast with a kind of whiplash effect. Be sure that the children keep holding hands throughout!

Line dance
Age 7 and older
May be simplified as a circle dance for younger children

Sandgate

VERSE

As I came through Sand-gate, through Sand-gate, through Sand-gate, As I came through Sand-gate, I heard a las-sie sing. "Oh,

CHORUS

weel may the keel row, the keel row, the keel row,

Weel may the keel row, that my lad-die's in."

English

Sandgate is a coal town in Northumbria, England, near the Scottish border. The "keel rows" are flat-bottom boats used for transporting coal along the rivers and canals. "Weel" is an old Anglo-Saxon word meaning, "very well." I learned and loved this playful song as a child. When I became a teacher it came back to me, and I combined it with a favorite snatch of choreography. To begin, the children stand in two lines across from their partners, with hands joined and raised to form a long gateway. The song is repeated over and over again, as two by two the children process through the passage and out again to rejoin the standing structure.

AS I CAME THROUGH SANDGATE, THROUGH SANDGATE, THROUGH SANDGATE,
AS I CAME THROUGH SANDGATE, I HEARD A LASSIE SING.

Chorus
"OH, WEEL MAY THE KEEL ROW,
THE KEEL ROW, THE KEEL ROW,
WEEL MAY THE KEEL ROW,
THAT MY LADDIE'S IN."

Verse
"HE WEARS A BLUE BONNET,
BLUE BONNET, BLUE BONNET,
HE WEARS A BLUE BONNET,
A DIMPLE ON HIS CHIN."

The first couple bends down and travels through the long gateway to the far end. The couple emerges, and immediately finds their respective places on either side of the moving tunnel and raises their arms to rejoin the others. Meanwhile, the second couple is followed by the third, the fourth, and so, on creating a continuously moving and flexible tunnel. Starting at our classroom door, the children once gleefully danced *Sandgate* repeatedly across the playground to the far edge of the playing field.

Line and partner dance
Age 8 and older

Line Dances

Oranges and Lemons

"Oran - ges and lem - ons," say the bells of Saint Clem - ent's. "You owe me five far - things," say the bells of Saint Mar - tin's. "When will you pay me?" say the bells of Old Bai - ley. "When I grow rich," say the bells of Shore - ditch. "When will that be?" say the bells of Step - ney. "I do not know," says the great bell of Bow. Here comes a can - dle to light you to bed, and here comes a chop - per to chop off your head.

English

In the perilous old City of London stand notable churches, each with its own distinctive bells. According to legend, all of these bells speak to one another, including the bell rung before the execution of criminals. In this centuries-old singing game, we hear the bells parlaying. To begin the game, two children raise their joined hands together to form an arch. Each has secretly determined whether to be "oranges" or "lemons." The others form a line, and walk through the arch. Everyone sings:

"ORANGES AND LEMONS," SAY THE BELLS OF SAINT CLEMENT'S.
"YOU OWE ME FIVE FARTHINGS," SAY THE BELLS OF SAINT MARTIN'S.
"WHEN WILL YOU PAY ME?" SAY THE BELLS OF OLD BAILEY.
"WHEN I GROW RICH," SAY THE BELLS OF SHOREDITCH.
"WHEN WILL THAT BE?" SAY THE BELLS OF STEPNEY.
"I DO NOT KNOW," SAYS THE GREAT BELL OF BOW.
HERE COMES A CANDLE TO LIGHT YOU TO BED,
AND HERE COMES A CHOPPER TO CHOP OFF YOUR HEAD.

On the word HEAD of the last line, the two children who have formed the arch, drop their hands over the child in the archway or the nearest child. Privately, the captured children are asked by the whispering archway which side they will join, "oranges" or "lemons." According to their decision, they move to one side or the other of the arch and hold on to the growing line. As the song ends and all have been captured and decided to go one way or the other, there is a tug-of-war. Even though the sides may be unequal in number, at a signal from a designated leader, the tug begins.

Line game
Age 5 and older

Line Dances

Noble Duke of York

Oh, the no-ble Duke of York, He had ten thou-sand men. He marched them up to the top of the hill, and he marched them down a-gain.

English

At the very beginning of the 20th century in England, it is recorded that long processions of couples marched and rollicked up and down the hillsides to this song during the holidays. In my class we dance this singing game with our fathers during the Fathers' Day celebration. Although it spoofs the old Frederick, Duke of York, it still ignites enthusiasm and valor. To begin, two lines of dancers stand and face each other. Everyone sings:

Verse one:
OH, THE NOBLE DUKE OF YORK,
HE HAD TEN THOUSAND MEN.
HE MARCHED THEM UP TO THE TOP OF THE HILL,
AND HE MARCHED THEM DOWN AGAIN.
Verse two:
AND WHEN YOU'RE UP, YOU'RE UP.
AND WHEN YOU'RE DOWN, YOU'RE DOWN.
AND WHEN YOU'RE ONLY HALFWAY UP,
YOU'RE NEITHER UP NOR DOWN.

The first couple in line is called "the head couple." They join hands and "sashay," sliding down to the far end of the line and back to their places. The head woman peels to the right as the head man peels to the left. They lead their respective lines down to the end, where they meet to join hands and form an arch. All the other couples bow under this arch and proceed up to the top of the line, where there is now a new head couple. The old head couple remains at the bottom far end of the line.

Line dance
Age 7 and older

A-Hunting We Will Go

A - hunt-ing we will go, A - hunt-ing we will go. We'll
catch a fox, and put him in a box, and then we'll let him go.

English

The oldest stories and songs often carry many layers of meaning. In our growing urban landscapes, the well-being of foxes is in peril, just as foxes always have been at risk when hunters are about. Nowadays there is ever-increasing cause for concern and compassion for animals. The foxy part of our minds relishes intrigue and cunning, yet the answers are not always found in cunning. We must often learn to think and move "outside the box." To begin this singing game, the children form two lines facing one another. Everyone sings:

A-HUNTING WE WILL GO,
A-HUNTING WE WILL GO.
WE'LL CATCH A FOX, AND PUT HIM IN A BOX,
AND THEN WE'LL LET HIM GO.

This game is played like *The Noble Duke of York*. In fact, in the early 1900s it was customary to add this song onto it. One can sing *A-Hunting We Will Go* to provide additional and appropriate musical measures, as the couples progress underneath the archway and back to their places. When all have returned, and the new head couple is in place, the game resumes with *The Noble Duke of York*.

To extend the song for dancing and for fun, one can invent verses with various animals: CATCH A RAT AND PUT HIM IN A HAT AND THEN WE'LL LET HIM GO, CATCH A FLEA AND PUT HIM IN A TREE, etc. An older version of this song insists at the end: WE'LL CATCH A FOX AND PUT HIM IN A BOX AND NEVER LET HIM GO. Where the hunt was an honorable necessity, this old wording makes sense. And indeed, there are times when we must keep our wits about us!

Line game
Age 7 and older

Line Dances

Bro, Bro Breda

Bro, bro bre - da, the clock has struck e - lev - en.

We can see in his cas - tle grand the king so bold - ly stand, As white as

chalk, as black as coal. Hur - ry up, my sol - dier, your life is in great dan - ger.

He who comes at the ver - y end, Shall all his days in the ket - tle spend.

First time we shall let him go, sec - ond time he may pass al - so.

When the third time he comes by, We'll throw him in the ket - tle.

Danish

Children naturally participate, in their own ways, in the mysteries of good and evil and right and wrong. The tug between opposites is re-enacted in this game. It is based upon an old Scandinavian tale about a king who has made a lamentable choice: as his subjects cross a new bridge, the king has agreed that the last one to cross will forfeit his life as payment and be "thrown into the kettle." Once captured, this last one in line each time joins the archway children to strengthen the bridge. When everyone has become evenly distributed on both sides of the bridge, a tug-of-war ensues. Then the game begins again.

BRO, BRO BREDA,
THE CLOCK HAS STRUCK ELEVEN.
WE CAN SEE IN HIS CASTLE GRAND
THE KING SO BOLDLY STAND,
AS WHITE AS CHALK, AS BLACK AS COAL.
HURRY UP, MY SOLDIER,
YOUR LIFE IS IN GREAT DANGER.
HE WHO COMES AT THE VERY END,
SHALL ALL HIS DAYS IN THE KETTLE SPEND.
FIRST TIME WE SHALL LET HIM GO,
SECOND TIME HE MAY PASS ALSO.
WHEN THE THIRD TIME HE COMES BY,
WE'LL THROW HIM IN THE KETTLE.

Two children stand facing each other and join their hands to make an archway. The other children form a line and pass under the arch. As the last line of the song is sung, the archway children drop their joined hands on the word KETTLE to capture the child who is passing underneath at that moment. The captured child holds onto the shoulders of one of the archway children. Subsequent captives alternate between one side and the other, until there are two lines of children. The two children who first made the archway grasp each other's wrists as their lines hold onto one another, and pull at a designated signal from the teacher.

Line dance
Age 7 and older

Alabama Gal

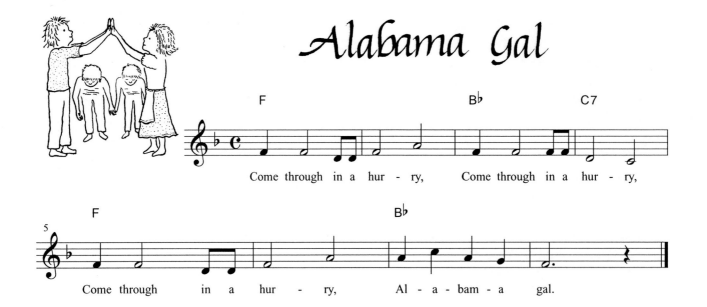

F   B♭   C7

Come through in a hur - ry,   Come through in a hur - ry,

F   B♭

Come through   in a hur - ry,   Al - a - bam - a   gal.

American

Singing Games

Singing games like this one prepare children for two-line American contra dancing. Across the United States, countless people of all ages gather regularly to practice these socially dynamic traditional dances. In crowded church halls, scout houses, community centers, and anywhere with a sturdy floor, contra dancing creates a robust feeling of joy. It requires partners who face one another who progress through different forms. To begin this dance, the partners stand in two equal lines:

COME THROUGH IN A HURRY,
COME THROUGH IN A HURRY,
COME THROUGH IN A HURRY,
ALABAMA GAL.

The first couple in line meets in the middle, joins hands and slides ("sashays") down to the far end of the line and back again.

I DON'T KNOW HOW, HOW,
I DON'T KNOW HOW, HOW,

All place their right palm on their partner's right palm. Holding their palms high, they circle once around.

I DON'T KNOW HOW, HOW,
ALABAMA GAL.

All place their left palm on their partner's left palm. Holding their palms high, they circle once around.

I'LL SHOW YOU HOW...
AIN'T I ROCK CANDY...

The first couple in line "casts off." The child on the right peels off to the right, and leads that line down to the bottom of the line as the child on the left peels off to the left and leads that line down to the bottom. Then the top couple meets at the bottom and forms an arch. The rest of the children meet their partners, as they stoop under the arch and continue dancing toward the top to form two lines again. Now there is a new top couple. The old top couple remains at the bottom. Continue the dance until all the couples have sashayed, cast off, and formed the arch.

Contra dance
Age 7 and older

A Message for Teachers

Anna and I met in 1992 when I first attended her singing games workshop at the annual Northern California Kindergarten Conference. I continued to participate in her inspirational workshops during the next decade—her supply of games seemed endless. Not a week has gone by during these many years that I have not taught my class some singing games. Sometimes the children beg for particular ones. "Can't we do *Old Roger Is Dead* once more?" they plead. I often discover the children during recess enjoying singing games on their own, or humming the tunes as they skip into the classroom.

Singing games are not just entertainment. Their educational purpose goes beyond the children's enjoyment. Holistic methods strive to integrate the mind and the emotions with physical activities that are rooted in history. The singing games in this book often hold spiritual significance as well. For example, the inner pictures of *Sally Go 'Round the Sun* portray the incarnation of a child's soul into his or her physical body at birth. Such pictures resonate deep into children and can have a healing and helping effect as they match the age development of the child.

Many traditions have arisen in my classroom and school because of the games that Anna Rainville presents in this book. The singing games offer a way for us to celebrate the seasons of the year together. Today the students and teachers in our whole school dance our way through the year. In my class we often begin with *Floating Down the River* and weaving a harvest wreath together. With the onset of winter, it's "Yo ho, yo ho, yo ho, There stands a man of snow." In spring we merrily dance around the maypole. Regular rhythmic singing and dancing together brings the experience of seasonal changes right down into our limbs, fingers and toes.

Singing games offer true healing for this materialistic, mechanistic age. In our largely urban society, it is especially important for children—and adults along with them—to learn to dance and sing together. I believe that children who participate in these musical games with a group of friends will recover much of the vitality they may lose by working on a computer or watching television.

Recently I led Anna's New Year singing game *Ring It In* with my whole school. The group included kindergarteners through eighth-graders, as well as teachers. Every child participated, and everyone loved dancing together in a mood of celebration.

Yes, both teachers and students need and deserve singing games! It is with great delight that I invite you to dive into the book you have in your hands and to begin to share the singing games you learn from it with both the children and adults whom you know. If you can't figure out a melody or forget a tune, you can do what Anna Rainville has invited all her adult students to do: Call me and I will sing the song for you.

James W. Peterson
Canyon School, California
author of *The Secret Life of Kids*

Left to right: Lee Anne Welch, Helen Caswell, Anna Rainville

About the Collaborators

Anna Rainville

Anna Rainville has been singing, dancing and teaching all her life. She has taught in the United States and abroad. Her life's mission has been to promote and teach the values and philosophy of Waldorf education, a task she has been engaged in since receiving her Master's Degree in Waldorf Education from Adelphi University in 1979. Anna has taught movement and singing games for teachers for several years at Rudolf Steiner College. She now is a class teacher at the Waldorf School of the Peninsula, in Los Altos, California. In recognition of her excellence as a teacher and her dedication to early child-hood education, the California Kindergarten Association presented her with the Audrey Sanchez Teacher Enhancement Award in 2002. In 1989 she was named Teacher of the Year by the Lakeside Joint Elementary School District in Los Gatos, California. She is a co-founder and co-director of the Kindergarten Forum and is on the Board of the National Kindergarten Alliance. In her view of the world, every moment is a chance to sing and to dance.

Helen Caswell

Helen Caswell is a beloved and prolific artist whose portraits and murals are featured in both corporate and private collections. Her most recent projects are for a stained glass window in the Methodist Church in Sebastopol and murals for Villa Sienna in Redwood City and St. Ignatius Church in San Francisco. Helen has taught classes and workshops in both writing and painting and served as artist-in-residence at centers in New Hampshire and Michigan. She also has created text and illustrations for over 30 books. She owns her own stone lithography press, and during the past few years she has begun working in watercolor. Born in California, she grew up in Oregon and attended the University of Oregon, majoring in fine arts. Helen Caswell now lives on a farm in Sebastopol, California, a gracious hostess, surrounded by generations of her family.

Lee Anne Welch

Lee Anne Welch's musical life has intertwined with that of Anna Rainville and Helen Caswell and their families since childhood. In college Lee Anne and Anna started their collaboration as "Fiddle and Quill," an association that continues to this day. At the Caswells' home, in the foothills of the Santa Cruz Mountains near where she lives and teaches today, Lee Anne was introduced to the hospitality of Celtic celebrations, with music and dancing until dawn. After Lee Anne graduated as a music major from the University of California at Santa Cruz, she began teaching violin and fiddle in earnest. Her goal was always to bring music to her students not as much as performance, but as a celebration. She has inspired multitudes of students to give their gifts with community-spirited warmth and verve. She is a founding member of the bluegrass band, Sidesaddle and Company, which has played steadily together since 1979, traveling widely across the US and Canada. Her fiddling is well-known to San Francisco Bay area contradancers.

Bibliography and Resources

Aulie, Jennifer and Margret Meyerkort. 1999. A series of six books: *Spring. Summer. Autumn. Winter. Spindrift. Gateways.* Wynstones Press: Stourbridge, UK

Bley, Edgar S. 1964. *The Best Singing Games for Children of All Ages.* Sterling Publishing Co., Inc.: NY

Baldwin Dancy, Rahima. 1989. *You are Your Child's First Teacher.* Celestial Arts: Berkeley, CA

Brooking-Payne. Kim. 1996. *Games Children Play.* Hawthorn Press: Stroud, UK

Chase, Richard. 1972. *Old Songs and Singing Games.* Dover: New York

Choksy, Lois. 1999. *The Kodaly Method I: Comprehensive Music Education.* Prentice Hall: New Jersey

Choksy, Lois and Richard Brummitt. 1987. *120 Singing Games and Dances for Elementary Schools.* Prentice Hall, Inc.: Englewood Cliffs, NJ

Davis, Andy, Peter Amidon, and Mary Cay Brass. 1997. A series of four books: *Jump Jim Joe: Great Singing Games for Children. Down in the Valley: More Great Singing Games for Children. Chimes of Dunkirk: Great Dances for Children. More Great Dances for Children.* New England Dancing Masters Productions: Brattleboro, VT

Foster, Nancy. 1999. *Dancing as We Sing: Seasonal Circle Plays and Traditional Singing Games for Young Children.* Acorn Hill Waldorf Kindergarten and Nursery: Silver Spring, MD

Gell, Heather. 1944. *Music, Movement and the Young Child.* Australasian Publishing Co.: Sydney, Australia

Goddard-Blythe, Sally. 2005. *The Well Balanced Child* (2nd edition). Hawthorn Press: Stroud, UK

Gomme, Alice. 1984. *The Traditional Games of England, Scotland and Ireland.* Thames and Hudson: New York

Goodkin, Doug. 2002. *Play, Dance and Sing: an introduction to Orff Schulwerk.* Schott: New York

Hallworth, Grace and Caroline Binch. 1996. *Down by the River: Afro-Caribbean Rhymes, Games and Songs for Children.* New York: Scholastic

Hannaford, Carla. 1995. *Smart Moves: Why learning is not all in your head.* Great Ocean Publishers: Arlington, VA

Jones, Bessie and Bess Lomax Hawes. 1972. *Step It Down: Games, Plays, Songs and Stories from the Afro-American Heritage.* University of Georgia Press: Athens, Georgia

Kerlee, Paul. 1994. *Welcome in the Spring: Morris and Sword Dances for Children.* World Music Press: Danbury, CT

Landeck, Beatrice. 1950. *Songs to Grow On.* Edward B. Marks Music Corporation: New York

———. 1954. *More Songs to Grow On.* Edward B. Marks Music Corporation: New York

Langstaff, John, George Emlen and Patrick Swanson. 2001. *Celebrate the Winter.* Revels, Inc. Publications: Watertown, MA

———. 1998. *Celebrate the Spring.* Revels, Inc. Publications: Watertown, MA

Langstaff, John and Nancy. 1986. *Sally Go Round the Moon.* Revels Publications: Cambridge, MA (originally published as *Jim Along Josie* by Harcourt Brace, 1970)

Lomax, Alan. 1975. *Folk Songs of North America.* Doubleday and Co.: Garden City, NY

Mattox, Cheryl Warren, 1990. *Shake It to the One You Love the Best: Play Songs and Lullabies from the Black Musical Tradition.* JTG: Nashville, TN

Mellon, Nancy. 1992. *Storytelling and the Art of Imagination.* Yellow Moon Press: Cambridge, MA

————. 2000. *Storytelling with Children.* Hawthorn Press: Stroud, UK.

Nelson, Esther. 1976. *Musical Games for Children of All Ages.* Sterling Publishing Co., Inc.: New York

Newell, William Wells. 1963. *Games and Songs of American Children.* Dover Publications, Inc.: New York

Opie, Iona and Peter. 1985. *The Singing Game.* Oxford University Press: Oxford, UK

Orozco, Jose-Luis, 1994. *De Colores and Other Latin-American Folk Songs for Children.* Dutton Children's Books: NY

Peck, Betty. 2005. *Kindergarten Education.* Hawthorn Press: Stroud, UK

Richards, Mary Helen. 1985. *Let's Do It Again! The Songs of Education Through Music.* Richards Institute of Music Education Research: Portola Valley, CA.

Rohrbaugh, Lynn. 1968. *Handy Play Party Book.* Cooperative Recreation Service: Delaware, Ohio

Seeger, Ruth Crawford. 1948. *American Folk Songs for Children.* Doubleday and Co.: Garden City, NY

Smyth, Nell. 2006. *Breathing Circle.* Hawthorn Press: Stroud, UK.

Steiner, Rudolf. 1974. *The Kingdom of Childhood.* Rudolf Steiner Press: London, UK

Von Heider, Molly. 1995. *Looking Forward.* Hawthorn Press: Stroud, UK

Van Haren, Will and Rudolf Kischnick. 1990. *Child's Play 1 & 2.* Hawthorn Press: Stroud, UK

Willwerth, Kundry. 1986. *Let's Dance and Sing: Story Games for Children.* Mercury Press: Spring Valley, NY

Music Education

American Orff-Schulwerk Association

Info@aosa.com

Dalcroze Society of America

www.dalcrozeusa.org.

Organization of American Kodaly Educators

www.oake.org

Resources

The American Folk Song Collection: an online resource of the Kodaly Center for Music Education at Holy Names University, Oakland, CA

http://kodaly.hnu.edu

Association of Waldorf Schools of North America: education support services

www.awsna.org

Country Dance and Song Society: books, recordings, morris bells, etc.

Office@cdss.org

New England Dancing Masters: books, recordings, dance instruction

Info@dancing masters.com

Kindergarten Forum: quarterly gatherings on kindergarten pedagogy

www.Kindergarten-forum.com

Revels: traditional folk music, dance and rituals from around the world

Info@revels.org

Rudolf Steiner College: Waldorf teacher training

www.steinercollege.edu

Index by Title

Index by First Line

CD Track Numbers

In keeping with the folk tradition, there may be slight variation between the printed lyrics and those on the CD.